WORK, AGE AND LEISURE

MICHAEL JOSEPH BOOKS ON

LIVE ISSUES

Series Editors H. L. Beales, O. R. McGregor

Work, Age and Leisure

CAUSES AND CONSEQUENCES OF THE SHORTENED WORKING LIFE

F. LE GROS CLARK, MA

London
MICHAEL JOSEPH

First published in Great Britain by
MICHAEL JOSEPH LIMITED
26 Bloomsbury Street
London, W.C.1
1966

Set and printed in Great Britain by
Unwin Brothers Limited at the Gresham Press, Woking,
in Imprint type, eleven-point leaded, and bound by
James Burn at Esher, Surrey

NOTE

Though the author is alone responsible for any conclusions reached in this study, he cannot but be grateful for the consistent help he has received from Officers of the General Register Office, the Ministry of Labour, the Ministry of Health and the Ministry of Pensions and National Insurance. His acknowledgements are also due to the Medical and Personnel Officers of many industrial undertakings, to Trade Union Officers and Sociologists in the U.S.A., and to the numerous individuals who made their time free for consultation. The secretarial assistance given in preparing the material has been indispensable, and especially that of Mrs T. Bloomberg who saw the work through from its inception. The study was carried out by means of a research grant from the Trustees of The Nuffield Foundation, London.

CONTENTS

Outline 9

1. Introductory—The Emergence of a Retirement Problem 13
2. Statistical Evidence for the New Trend 24
3. Industrial Setting for a Policy of Retirements 37
4. The Ultimate Test of an Older Man's Employability 50
5. Economic Pressures Round the Close of the Working Life 60
6. The assumption that Alternative Jobs must be Available 69
   (1) In Manufacturing Industries 69
7. The Assumption that Alternative Jobs must be Available 77
   (2) In Non-Manufacturing Industries 77
   Annotation to Chapters 6 and 7. Relevance of the Increasing Use of 'Light Work' in Industrial Rehabilitation 94
8. The Effect of Shifting the Physical Work-Load on to Machinery 101
9. The Health Status of Men of Pensionable Age 109
10. The Social Problems Implicit in a Policy of Retirements 117
    Annotation to Chapter 10. A Commentary on U.S. Experience 136
11. New Approaches to the Retirement Problem 143

Index 152

OUTLINE

One of the consequences of industrial growth is the tendency of firms to retire their manual employees at some pre-determined age. Its causes need to be analysed; it is shown here to be implicit in the gradual working out of the laws of economic progress. The sources of statistical evidence for the trend are critically examined. While they do not yet allow of any firm conclusion, they appear to reflect long-term changes in employment practices and policies.

We are not concerned in this study to measure the precise rate at which new techniques are likely to be assimilated into the structures of industry. We limit ourselves therefore to a description of their main characteristics, and to speculating about their effect in regard to the selection, organisation and retirement of manual workers. An inquiry is then undertaken into the factors that would decide whether or not an older employee is still fit to continue on his normal job. The decision is shown to be closely related in modern industry to the organising functions of a supervisory staff; it is the foreman who is most immediately concerned with production costs and with maintaining output. The significance of this relationship has, it is suggested, been too often overlooked, when the length of a man's working life is under discussion. The wider economic pressures, to which supervisors and workers are alike subjected, are also examined. They are seen to have a direct bearing on the preference for some pre-determined age of retirement.

Allowing that ageing employees have frequently to be taken

off their normal jobs, it is commonly assumed that industrial undertakings have still a reserve of alternative or 'light' work, to which they could be then transferred. To test this assumption, inquiries were made in a number of manufacturing and non-manufacturing concerns. The provisional conclusion reached is that the field of such 'light' work is not only small in relation to the increasing number of older applicants, but is almost certainly contracting. Some of the causes of such a contraction are identified and discussed; among them is the increasing practice of reserving 'light' jobs for the medical rehabilitation of convalescent employees. This is only one illustration of the regard now paid to the welfare of the younger men at work—to the implied disadvantage of men who have become pensionable. Another widely held assumption is that the process of ageing reveals itself in the manual worker through gradual changes in his muscles, joints and sense organs; an inference is that the average working life will be prolonged in the degree to which his physical work-load is shifted on to machinery. Some of the reasons for doubting this belief are discussed. It now seems not improbable that the demands made by automatic or semi-automatic installations will be an even more exacting test of a man's continued psychological reliability than has been manipulative work of an old operative's physical endurance and speed.

But meanwhile medical and sociological evidence is accumulating to suggest that the health of men in the early years of retirement remains on average unimpaired; most of them are for their age still mobile, competent and active-minded. Studies of the subjective attitudes of such older men about their retirement seem to confirm the general opinion that an indeterminate proportion of them become restless and ill-at-ease with so complete a suspension of the normal rhythms of their working life. It is the men of this temperamental type, who constitute the essence of the social dilemma. Accordingly, a critical review is undertaken of some of the schemes that have been promoted by various agencies for giving pensioners a

1 Introductory – The Emergence of a Retirement Problem

We often hear it said that accelerated changes in industrial methods must have social consequences beyond the sphere of industry. I want now to discuss one of these consequences. It is the effect that industrial progress is having upon the average age at which men are retired from work. In the long run the trend will set up a series of new social problems. To avoid any misunderstanding I will quote in substance from the findings of an International Scientific Seminar, that was held at Stockholm in 1962 by the Organisation for Economic Co-operation and Development. The subject matter of the Seminar was 'Age and Employment'.[1]

The participants in the Seminar came to the conclusion that three distinct problems can be identified; though these problems are inter-related and overlap with one another, economists should give each of them separate attention.

(1) There is the effect that recent accelerations in the rate of technological change are likely to have for men and women who are a little beyond the mid point of their working lives (i.e. those, broadly speaking, between the ages of 40 and 55 or so); the effect will be one of an increased stress and will include the complex difficulties implicit in re-training and re-settling them.

(2) There is the transitional phase around the usual pensionable age; this is a phase in which men and women are, in general, still capable of socially useful work (whether remunerated or voluntary), while probably no longer fully effective in what had been their normal employment.

(3) There is the phase—essentially a new one for most

[1] O.E.C.D., 2, Rue Andre Pascal, Paris. 1962.

manual workers—in which a number of years must be spent in complete or virtual retirement.

It is with the last two of these problems that I propose to deal. The first is now receiving a good deal of attention elsewhere. There has indeed been a noticeable shift of Ministerial interest lately towards the problems of redundancy. For with the varying amounts of contraction and expansion that are taking place in industry the Government finds itself involved in re-training schemes and the possible transfer of workers from one part of the country to another. Moreover, there is always the difficulty of deciding for what jobs a middle-aged man shall be trained, since that must depend on economic forecasts. One American writer (now on the staff of O.E.C.D.) was making the point five years ago.[1] For him the 'older person' evidently meant such as were over 45 or so. 'We have', he said, 'to combine economic policies stimulating high economic activity with programmes for the generation of jobs designed to meet the special needs of people unabsorbed by the high levels of economic activity. We have to create direct job-making activities along with the promotion of new enterprises for the nation as a whole.'

Let me here say in passing that with this recent shift of interest there is some risk that our terminology may become hopelessly confused. The use of the term 'older worker' is quite permissible, provided the writer makes it clear what chronological age he has in mind. But a survey of the literature shows that some, and often without specifying it, are discussing all workers from about 45 upwards, while others make it plain that they are concerned only with those who are nearing or passing their pensionable age. The term should therefore be applied sparingly; and when I use it, it can be taken to mean no man below the age of 60.

For the sake of simplicity I shall confine myself to the male manual worker, and to the social and economic conditions that

[1] S. Barkin, 'Fitting jobs to the Unemployed Older Person'. Address before the National Council of the Ageing, U.S.A. 1961.

affect his final withdrawal from what had hitherto been his normal job. I shall not attempt to solve the personal or financial problems that may be engendered for him by his withdrawal.

As a matter of fact, much of what I have to say will reflect an industrial bias. I want to analyse the complex causes of this new social dilemma. We must be clear about the limited role of industrial managers and trade unionists. Their function is that of seeing to the deployment and the welfare of such men and women as are currently in the labour force; their responsibilities do not extend to those who had to leave the labour force by reason of age or chronic invalidity. They may admit individually (or even collectively) to some residual obligation for their continued well-being; but in practice they can do little to implement that obligation beyond undertaking to pay them an industrial pension.

As far as they are concerned, the personal and domestic well-being of retired pensioners should be the business of non-industrial agencies—and ultimately no doubt the business of Parliament itself. The mistake we make is to suppose that employers or trade unionists *as such* have duties that lie outside their special functions in an industrialised society; moreover, if there is to be technological change, they cannot long delay the related changes it brings about in manpower requirements and labour organisation.

It is as well to be plain from the start about the whole theme of this study. Men have always tended to think of the span of their lives as a series of stages—childhood, adolescence . . . early middle life, later middle life . . . and so on. The terms they used have varied; but the intention was the same. At no time could the age definitions have been absolutely precise. For example, in any large group of boys or girls the age at which puberty is reached will probably vary within a range of three or more years. But in practice the broad classifications hold good. Now, when we come to the later years of the life span, there seems to be an obsessive tendency among writers to throw together all men beyond, say, the conventional age of 65 and distinguish that period as 'old age'.

Of course, so long as writers define their terms clearly, they are free to make them mean what they wish—at all events within reason. But the trouble about the term 'old age' is that it carries so many overtones of dependence, weakness or passivity. *The sociological fact that I am here expounding is that for large numbers of men the life span beyond 65 or so now comprises not one but two definable phases.* Let me make a precise distinction between these two phases; as usual in human affairs it is a matter of proportionate numbers. When men have reached their mid sixties a noticeable and increasing *proportion* of them no longer meet the tests of working effectiveness imposed on them by modern industrial conditions. In a simpler industrial or pre-industrial economy that might not have been the case; but nowadays it is the case. Such men have to relinquish their normal jobs or moderate their efforts.

The second turning point is only reached when a significant *proportion* of elderly men begin to need constant aid and support from members of their households and/or the Health and Welfare Services. Medical evidence suggests that this proportion does not become significant or increase very steeply, until men are approaching their mid seventies. That may be properly described as the passage into true 'old age'.

In the nature of things there are in both cases plenty of overlapping and marginal areas. But if we concentrate upon the proportions that would be likely to strike managers or administrators, then we can say that at each of these two turning points the critical stage would come where at least 25–30 per cent of men are identified as needing (or likely soon to need) serious attention. There would be little doubt in their minds that thereafter the numbers will increase rapidly.

In consequence it is becoming rare for a man to be precipitated out of his working life into immediate and complete old age. On the contrary, there comes for the majority of men a kind of *intermediate* period of life, for which we have as yet no descriptive term. Such a period may last for five or ten years or longer; and for those who enter it the phase may be one of great import. It is in the nature of a lower plateau in the life span; and what I am affirming is that it is also in danger of being an unconsidered limbo.

The causes lie in the gradual working out of the economic laws of industrial growth. If we must have industrial progress, this is one of its inevitable by-products. The dilemma might be summed up in this way. In the more remote past it had almost always been possible to let a man moderate his efforts or change his style of work as soon as the years began to tell. The advance of mechanisation made this progressively less practicable. Industry has now reached a point at which the dilemma is becoming self-evident; manufacture and transport cannot economically absorb more than a small proportion of their human wastage, i.e. the 'marginal' types of labour embodied in many of their older employees. The result has been the creation of an extended 'no man's land', lying between the close of a man's normal working life and the time when true old age at last supervenes. We shall be examining some of its causes and characteristics.

The old economies of Europe were the domain of peasant farmers and handicraftsmen, of the masters of small weaving sheds, tanneries, metal working undertakings etc., and of the household and estate servants of large manors. It must not be supposed that under such conditions senescence was never an uncomfortable period of a man's life. There would frequently have been disputes about the transfer of farm holdings or the control of a workshop. When Shakespeare made an old serving man speak of 'unregarded age in corners thrown', he presumably knew that a Tudor audience would take the reference.[1] But the real point is that in that type of economy there were no

[1] *As You Like It*, Act 2, Scene 3.

inherent *technical* or *organisational* factors, that would have been a barrier to the continued employment of an older man; there were usually plenty of light tasks to be carried out. Besides, social and family customs recognised the mutual rights and duties between successive generations and, for the matter of that, those prevailing between master and man. What would have struck a community was the occasional callousness shown by a son or by a landed proprietor.

The consciousness of the nineteenth century, that industrialism had changed all this, took various forms. But it mainly inclined to think in terms of an industrial pension. The Victorians were well acquainted with the systems in use for pensioning off civil servants and members of the Armed Forces. In 1858 Ruskin was declaring that, 'it ought to be as natural for a labourer to take his pension from the parish for work well done as it is for a man in higher rank'. But to the end of the century there survived an awareness that the nature of a man's occupation and of his social environment were really the important factors. Charles Booth, one of the promotors of the campaign that led to the passing of the first Pensions Act in this country (1908) seems clear about this.[1] What he said in substance was that the country has an advantage over the town at every point. There is in town less work suitable for old men; and in urban pursuits a loss of capacity precedes the actual loss of strength. 'Men in town life', he added, 'are thrown early out of work. The old are comparatively at a disadvantage owing to the increased stress of industrial life. The improvement in industrial conditions thus acts directly against and only indirectly in favour of the old.'

We may no doubt assume that it is happiest for a man when he can withdraw from work in his own time and at his own pace. But that is only possible in the full sense when he is working for himself or in an intimate family group. To study such uncomplicated working conditions, we should presumably

[1] Charles Booth, *Old Age Pensions and the Aged Poor* (Foreword), London, 1899.

have to go back to a pre-industrial economy; and for that we have in this country no statistical evidence. Our only sources of information, curiously enough, are the Census Reports for 1951 and 1961. For National Insurance purposes the Registrar General undertook in 1951 to prepare a Table analysing by age and occupation all the persons who recorded themselves as being 'self-employed'. Such a Table had never been published before; but the terms of it were repeated (possibly with slight variations) in the 1961 Report.

In earlier Census Reports only the total number of such persons had been indicated. In 1951 the number of men, who stated that they were working 'on their own account' was 841,856. The number in 1931 had been 835,437. So a man's chances of making a living in this way seem to have remained fairly constant. In 1961 the number had apparently fallen to 721,930; but this may have been due to more precise instructions given by the Registrar General. The 1961 figures may be the more reliable. These men and their jobs can therefore be taken as representing the belated survivals among us from a pre-industrial economy; and we may ask how far senescence had been affecting their capacity to remain at work.

The Table that follows lists a few of these 'self-employed' occupations. It seems obvious from the Census Reports that comparatively few of the men had been working on their own account before the age of 30. Moreover, some men evidently quit industry in middle life and set up as small shopkeepers, watch repairers and the like. I have therefore taken only the numbers of men who were aged 30 and upwards, and shown what proportions of them were over 65 in 1951 and 1961. These percentages give some indication of the relative chances they had of working on into near old age.

To bring into relief the meaning of these proportions we have only to contrast with them the proportions of men of similar ages in contemporary manufacture. I took a series of industrial occupations as shown in the 1961 Census Report: those of foundrymen, sheet metal workers, welders, workers in

Table I

PROPORTIONS OF MEN OVER 65 IN CERTAIN SELF-EMPLOYED OCCUPATIONS

(Total numbers being men over 30)

Men working on their own account as	*Percentages 65 and over in all men aged 30 and over*	
	1951	*1961*
Small farmers, nurserymen, etc.	13·4	11·3
Jobbing gardeners and the like	20·8	17·1
Shoe repairers	16·8	15·0
Watch repairers	14·0	21·0
Barbers	11·1	12·7
Tailors and garment makers	22·0	19·8
Small shop-keepers (non-food)	14·2	11·4

gas, coke and chemicals, wood machinists, upholsterers and paper makers. The same yardstick was applied to them, i.e. it was asked what proportion of the men aged 30 and over were 65 and over. The percentages varied in these cases from about 0·8 to about 4·8 with a concentration around 2·0.

This is probably about as far as we can go in attempting to compare statistically the past with the present. The figures give us perhaps the only opportunity we have of reducing such distinctive working conditions to some semblance of a pattern. Between the two contrasting groups of figures there lie, as it were, the changes that have been taking place throughout our industrial history.

The nineteenth century had been aware that industrialisation was slowly converting those who were unemployed simply by reason of their age into special cases of pauperism. But it was not until the Census of 1901 that any serious attempt was officially made to discover how many they were and from what jobs they had come. When new questions are included on a Census Form, it usually means that a Government Department is in need of statistical information. By 1901 the agitation for an Old Age Pension was well under way. The reformers found ample support in the House of Commons; and since a Bill of some kind would probably have to be debated, its financial implications had better be studied. As it happens, the published Tables of 1901 were not at all reliable. It seems clear, for one thing, that the very term 'retired' was still construed by many people as a mark of status. Government servants, e.g. from the armed forces, police, coastguards etc., were known to reach a retirement age; the description was not felt by the public to be appropriate for the common run of industrial workers.

About 93,100 men aged 65–74 recorded themselves in 1901 as 'retired'; and according to the Table few of these could have been in receipt of a pension. Since there were only about 22 of them to every 100 men, who could claim to be still at work, the figures are likely to be an understatement. From some industries, such as mining, building and rail transport, the recorded numbers of 'retired' were (by Census admission) almost incredibly low. It was thought that many such men might have been classified indifferently in the Census as labourers; and the fact that at the time a proportion of elderly men were workhouse inmates lends some colour to this assumption. Workhouses contained 8·3 per cent of retired men of the ages 65 to 74, and almost a quarter of those aged 75 and over.

By the time of the 1931 Census the statistics were becoming a little more reliable. With the gradual spread of industrial superannuation schemes the notion of a retirement was more generally accepted. But even today the figures are in all probability under-stated. People are instructed on a Census Form to say whether they are 'wholly retired'; and that could mean that a number, who had taken up their State pensions but had continued in some alternative part time employment, did not record themselves as retired. Technically, however, they would have been retired *from their normal jobs*; and that, after all, is what primarily counts with a man.

We must remember, then, that only of late years has *retirement* been part of a working man's vocabulary. The word had always borne somewhat of an honorific connotation. Cromwellian officers, for instance, are known to have been placed 'on the retired list'; and so doubtless were many persons of rank before and since that time. But for an old working man of the nineteenth century and even well beyond, all that happened would have been that his periods of unemployment grew more protracted, until at last he stopped looking for a job altogether.

Much of this study will be given over to an analysis of the economic causes of the problem. But towards its close I shall turn to consider what are the mental attitudes and the physical status of men when first they are retired from employment. That will give us at least a provisional idea of the manner of men with whom we are concerned. The essence of the matter is, I think, that we shall soon find it necessary to treat retirement (at all events in its early stages) as a comprehensive way of life with its own unique code of social rights. For it will often represent a long period of time and will embrace a large section of the population. In the final issue some public authority has always to make itself responsible for remedying the social maladjustments, that have been generated in the course of industrial growth.

As for the overall dimensions of the problem, I do not expect them to impress immediately those who are continually immersed in day-to-day industrial affairs; their minds move, as it were, in a different element. But there are perhaps two or three arguments to which we could appeal. It is noticeable, for instance, that the attitudes of men about an inevitable retirement frequently change as the critical moment approaches. What had seemed a welcome relief in prospect becomes gradually far less attractive; and a policy-maker in his prime of life had better take this psychological fact into consideration. Again, it could be pointed out that, once a man has made the transition from work, what he then does with his life is liable to seem quite as important to him as had seemed his period of employment; to prepare himself for his new experience is elementary common sense. Lastly, it appears to me that a fair number of families go through a phase of anxiety about the emotional condition of some recently retired member; to put it briefly, the ageing man is by no means happy. Many families are still closely knit, and such sources of domestic anxiety, when they do occur, are not altogether conducive to efficiency among the members of the working generation. I would go further and suggest that concern for the more or less avoidable worries of elderly relatives may well be in the aggregate one of the major causes of family uneasiness to-day.

Until recently manual workers withdrew from employment (in most instances) at ages and for reasons so varied, that no one thought the matter worth much attention. Indeed, no clear trends would probably have been observable. Nowadays we can no longer afford to let it rest at that. Our first task is to analyse the statistical material, that reflects the industrial setting within which the whole process is gradually unfolding itself; the process is reaching the stage at which we are beginning to notice a fundamental qualitative change in industrial outlook.

2 *Statistical Evidence for the New Trend*

The simplest way of meeting the social cost of large scale rationalisation in industry is to retire an increasing number of men at relatively early ages. That would amount to a method of maintaining an appearance of 'full employment'. We have first to see whether there is any statistical evidence that this is happening.

There are three main sources of information, i.e. the Occupation Tables of the Census Reports, the Industrial Tables that are published annually by the Ministry of Labour and the Tables published by the Ministry of Pensions and National Insurance. But before we go further, one point has to be cleared out of the way. Since we shall be dealing mainly with the period 1950–63, it is necessary to note that the men aged 60 and over in that period were of the generation affected by the 1914–18 war. Might that fact have had any influence upon their rates of retirement?

According to one estimate the British war deaths in 1914–18 were between 700,000 and 800,000; and, if we may judge from the age distribution of surviving war pensioners, some 70 per cent of these men must have been born between 1890 and 1899. In consequence there was a net loss of men from that generation as it moved on through the post-war decades. Thus the 1921 Census showed approximately 400,000 fewer men of the ages 20–29 than we might have expected if the numbers in that age group had increased smoothly from 1911. Again, in 1951 the men aged 50–59, who represented the same war-time generation, were about 500,000 short of what might have been expected, had there been no war. No doubt their numbers had been further depleted by post-war emigration.

By 1961 the members of the war-time generation were mostly aged 60–69; and here normal mortality was beginning to have a marked effect. The result of the original war losses was less evident. But in any case, could those losses have influenced the *proportions* of such older men who retired or remained at work?

By the year 1958 the men who had been born in the mid 'nineties (the peak of the war casualties) were approaching or passing the age of 65. At that point of time, whether or not it was a mere matter of coincidence, the rate of early retirements certainly seemed to rise; and we are still left with one residual question. Was the presence of so many surviving war pensioners an important element in advancing the *average* rate of retirement from the labour force? I shall examine this possibility a little later, when I come to Ministry of Labour statistics of employment.

The only sure method of analysing retirement trends is to see what *proportions* of older men are still being employed. To do this we have, of course, to relate the numbers of older men in the population to the numbers who are recorded as being at work. The Registrars General publish annual estimates of the male population in successive age groups; their annual estimates are based on Census Tables, as adjusted year by year.[1]

On the other hand, the Ministry of Labour's annual statistics of employment are based on a 1 per cent sample count of all insured persons. The figures include men who happen to be unemployed at the time or absent from work. But it must be noted that they do not include employers or men working on their own account; they are therefore not fully comprehensive. They would, for instance, differ a little from the figures shown in the Occupation Tables of the Census Reports. Moreover, any figures based on so small a sample are liable to statistical errors. For our present purpose this simply means that all relatively small year-to-year fluctuations in the percentages would have to be ignored; for they may be due to mere chance.

[1] Separate estimates are published for England and Wales and for Scotland. Table I is based on the combined figures.

Only when we come across decisive trends extending over a term of years, are we justified in taking the matter seriously.

The men of three age groups are here compared with one another—i.e. 60–64, 65–69 and 70 and over; the percentages show what proportions of them were apparently at work in each of the age groups in a series of years. The figures refer to the whole of Great Britain, since the Scottish population figures have been included in the computation.

Table II

APPROXIMATE PERCENTAGES OF MEN RECORDED AS BEING AT WORK IN THE UNITED KINGDOM IN THE YEARS AND AGE GROUPS INDICATED

		Age groups	
Year	*60–64*	*65–69*	*70 and over*
1952	87·5	48·5	19·0
1954	90·5	50·0	18·5
1956	92·0	53·5	20·0
1958	90·0	51·5	19·0
1960	89·0	45·0	17·5
1961	90·0	44·0	17·0
1962	91·0	41·0	17·0
1963	91·5	40·0	16·0

It can be taken, I think, that the rate of participation had remained relatively constant for men in their early sixties. Allowing for the fact that employers, etc., were not included in the numbers of men at work, we may assume that the *real* percentages would probably be somewhat higher. But it is commonly estimated that at this stage of life around 8 per cent of all men are in virtual retirement as a result of injury or chronic sickness; though that may be true, it is not necessarily reflected with precision in the Ministry of Labour figures. We can only say that there is no sign of men being retired as yet to any marked degree before the age of 65.

When, however, we come to the men in their late sixties, we find an apparent change in their rates of participation starting somewhere about 1958. By 1962 the percentage (at all events according to the Ministry of Labour) had fallen to 41·0, and in 1963 to about 40·0. With the men of 70 and over the figures follow the same trend. In precise terms, the population of the men of 70 and over *rose* over a decade by about 6·4 per cent, while the number of those who were at work had *declined* by 1963 in about the same proportion. Though it is probable that some employment changes had taken place in this age group by 1963, their full dimensions will not be clear until the early retirements have had ample time to influence the position among the men of later ages.

We have plainly to ask ourselves whether factors at work over the last few years have been tending to accelerate the withdrawal of men in their late sixties. A large proportion of such withdrawals always falls at the age of 65. It is conceivable, then, that if we knew what happens to men at the age of 65, we should see whether there really are economic forces compelling or persuading men to leave work at that age in greater numbers.

If we learn how many men of the age of 64 are at work in any mid-year, then it is certain that a year later they will all be 65; and those who were to leave employment on reaching that age would have gone. The proportion of losses from the labour force may thus be estimated. By applying the same period labour force may thus be estimated. By applying the same method over a term of years, we should see whether indeed there are any signs of a change in their retirement habits. Some men would have died in the course of each successive year; but we may assume, I think, that their mortality rates would have remained constant. Using this method of 'moving cohorts', Table III shows the percentage of losses experienced over a series of years.

The difficulty is that the only figures available are those from the Ministry of Labour's 1 per cent sample; and there is thus some risk of statistical errors. The level of losses might oscillate fairly widely around, say, 30 per cent without indicating that any real change had taken place. But a rise in losses to 40 per cent or more (especially if it persists) is probably significant.

Table III

NUMBERS OF EMPLOYED MEN (IN THOUSANDS) SHOWN AS 'COHORTS' MOVING FROM AGE 64 TO 65, AND THE APPROXIMATE PERCENTAGES OF LOSS FROM THE LABOUR FORCE DURING THE YEAR

Year	*Numbers at work aged 64 in the year indicated*	*Numbers at work aged 65 in the year following each year indicated*	*Per cent loss of numbers between ages 64 and 65*
1950	138	97	29
1951	133	98	26
1953	146	104	29
1955	153	112	27
1957	161	106	34
1959	152	92	39
1960	155	91	41
1961	161	85	47
1962	167	90	46
1963	170	87	49

The figures again suggest that somewhere in the late 'fifties a change was occurring in men's habits or in industrial policy. We can conjecture what this change may have implied. As to the residual effect of the 1914–18 war—the men who became 64 within the years 1957 and 1961 must have been born between 1893 and 1898. Now, it was men born in those years who represented about 44 per cent of all the war pensioners who had survived till 1961. It cannot be said, however, that the presence of so many war pensioners in the age group we are considering would have led to any perceptible rise in the rates of retirement. According to one estimate since the year 1957 they have made up only about 5–10 per cent of all men who reached the age of 65; and there are other grounds for supposing that they cannot greatly have influenced the overall levels of retirement. It is improbable, for instance, that more than a quarter of them had serious disablements, i.e. disablements classified as over 50 per cent. Moreover, a proportion of the most severely disabled war pensioners would not in any case have been gainfully occupied.

Nevertheless, the possible impact of the 1914–18 war on retirement rates cannot altogether be excluded. Some forms of disablement might have inclined a number of men to claim a State pension, as soon as they were entitled to draw it. Again, the original removal by death of several hundred thousand able-bodied young men could have lowered, however slightly, the average level of fitness in their generation; it is obvious, for instance, that many of those rejected for the Armed Forces in 1914–18 must have displayed some constitutional weakness. But though these factors may conceivably have contributed to the increase in retirements, I cannot believe that their effects were more than marginal. The real causes, in other words, were not historical but contemporary.

The Ministry of Pensions and National Insurance publishes Tables showing what numbers of men take up their State pensions in successive periods of time. The Tables further indicate what proportions had claimed pensions at 65 and at each subsequent year of age up to 70. At 70, it will be remembered, men can claim pensions, whether or not they then continue to work. These Tables naturally help us to trace apparent changes in retirement habits. But at the best they cannot be neatly fitted in with the figures published by the Ministry of Labour; and that for the simple reason that they cover categories of men who may not have been fully represented in the Ministry of Labour statistics. Any attempt to harmonise the two sets of figures might be misleading.

What has complicated the issue is the fact that in mid 1958 the field of men who are entitled to a pension was considerably widened. Though the number of applicants had previously been rising, as the numbers over 65 increased in the population, the level then rose suddenly by more than a sixth.

There is no need to explain in this context the regulations

governing the widening of the whole field of entitlement. The significant point to note is that a large proportion of the 'new style' claimants would have been among better paid non-manual workers; they would also have included a number of men who worked 'on their own account'. An indeterminate proportion of such men probably lay outside the Ministry of Labour statistics.

To judge from the Ministry of Pensions Tables, the change in regulations had at least the temporary result of shifting the age distribution of retirements; and it shifted it very markedly towards the age of 65. In some measure indeed the change in regulations may well have been a contributory cause in the shift. Table IV shows what proportions of the men, who claimed pension, were claiming it at 65 and at 70 in each of the years given; the remainder were, of course, distributed in each case over the four intervening years of a man's life.

Table IV

TOTAL NUMBERS OF MEN (IN THOUSANDS) CLAIMING PENSIONS IN THE YEARS INDICATED, AND THE PERCENTAGES OF THESE WHO CLAIMED AT 65 AND AT 70

Year	*Total number of awards (Males)*	*Percentages claiming at precise age*	
		65	*70*
1951	142·0	45·5	21·0
1954	150·7	42·4	19·9
1956	154·6	41·5	21·5
1957	159·0	41·4	20·4
1958	183·3	40·2	17·6
1959	208·8	45·3	14·0
1960	203·7	48·6	12·4
1961	188·3	53·5	12·6
1962	208·2	55·3	10·8
1963	212·7	53·5	9·6

We should probably be correct in surmising that many of the 'new style' claimants from 1958 were more disposed as a social class to retire at about 65. For instance, a large number of men of executive and managerial grades would be superannuated at about that age in any case; and self-employed men, not previously entitled to pension, might be inclined to take their pensions and then nominally limit their hours of work. All this would have the effect of shifting retirements a little towards the earlier end of the age scale. But does it account for the *whole* of the change that has taken place?

The proportion retiring at 65 had risen ultimately since 1956 by about 30 per cent; and the proportion who applied for pension at 70 (and in some cases no doubt continued to work) declined at the same time by 50 per cent. Now, it can be agreed that the influx of 'new style' claimants was bound to lead for a time to unpredictable fluctuations. But on the assumption that they have been increasing the annual number of *all* claimants by about a sixth, then the shifts from 1958 onwards seem too violent and continuous to be accounted for by this cause alone. At least half of the percentage changes emerging by 1962–3 must have been due, I think, entirely to changes in industrial practices and policies. In other words, they reflect precisely the same trends as those observable in the Ministry of Labour tables; and these latter, it will be recalled, have comparatively little to do with the widening of the field of entitlement.

The essence of the matter is that the age structure of a number of industries seems to be moving in a direction counter to changes in the age structure of the male population as a whole. While the total numbers 65 and over are steadily increasing, the working numbers are declining. Thus if we want the truth, we cannot rely upon overall figures alone. The Tables published annually by the Ministry of Labour break down the employment figures into a series of industrial catgories; and we have here to bear in mind that this is an *industrial* and not an occupational classification. That is to say, the figures usually include not only the skilled and semi-skilled manual workers but a variable proportion of clerical workers as well as such ancillary workers as messengers, canteen hands and cleaners. These last may in some instances represent a significant minority in an industry.

In analysing the age structure of the industries, the Ministry records only the numbers of older men who are *65 and over*; it does not break down their numbers more narrowly as it does in the case of the overall employed figures. Table V shows the

Table V

NUMBERS OF MEN AGED 65 AND OVER (IN THOUSANDS) STILL EMPLOYED IN SELECTED INDUSTRIES IN THE YEARS INDICATED

Industries	*1951*	*1956*	*1961*	*1962*	*1963*	*1964*
Agriculture	40	32	23	19	20	21
Coal Mining	25	22	2	1	2	2
Chemicals and Allied Industries	8	9	7	8	6	5
Metal Manufacture	18	19	15	12	12	9
Engineering, Shipbuilding and Electrical goods	51	63	46	45	43	42
Motor Vehicles	7	8	6	6	6	6
Textiles	24	25	20	17	16	15
Food, Drink and Tobacco	17	19	14	13	12	11
Building	43	40	30	30	28	31
Electricity	4	4	2	2	2	2
Railways	6	10	9	9	8	8
Road Motor Transport	8	8	10	9	10	10
Distributive Trades	44	59	61	57	58	56

Table VI

NUMBERS OF MEN OF ALL AGES (IN THOUSANDS) EMPLOYED IN THE SAME SELECTED INDUSTRIES IN THE YEARS INDICATED

Industries	*1951*	*1956*	*1961*	*1962*	*1963*	*1964*
Agriculture	673	538	464	441	429	405
Coal Mining	767	769	650	631	608	578
Chemicals and Allied Industries	343	375	387	380	377	371
Metal Manufacture	485	513	560	530	529	550
Engineering, Shipbuilding and Electrical goods	1,457	1,643	1,741	1,833	1,793	1,797
Motor Vehicles	256	283	359	373	393	419
Textiles	432	396	379	374	370	371
Food, Drink and Tobacco	471	494	458	470	471	466
Building	1,280	1,360	1,436	1,486	1,527	1,576
Electricity	162	178	190	197	203	206
Railways	486	463	413	405	381	362
Road Motor Transport	431	389	396	406	414	412
Distributive Trades	1,106	1,171	1,348	1,384	1,410	1,403

numbers of men of 65 and over estimated to have been at work in various industries; and it shows the numbers for a series of years. To complete the picture for the purpose of comparison, Table VI shows the total numbers of men *of all ages* in the same industries.

The significant point about these figures is the decline in the *proportions* of the men of 65 and over, rather than the decline in their absolute numbers. Their numbers have been rising in the population; yet only on the railways and in road transport have their proportions shown any temporary increase. In a few industries, e.g. chemicals and distribution, the proportion may have kept almost level with the growth in the total numbers employed. But in agriculture and building, the decline has been marked. The most extreme case is that of coal mining. The ruling that miners should be retired at 65 began to take effect in the first quarter of 1960; and this involved the withdrawal of around 12,000 men, whose ages of retirement might otherwise have been spread over a period of several years of life. How far this incident affected the level of the overall figures of retirement in 1960 (Table IV), it would be difficult to say. Its impact cannot have been entirely negligible.

The Tables seem to need one or two further comments. According to the Ministry of Agriculture the proportion of men over 65 in the industry did indeed decline between 1957 and 1962 from about 5·6 to 4·2 per cent of all male workers. This may have been due in part to an earlier drift away of the men in middle life. As for the men over 65, it appears that a quarter of them in 1963 were on part-time work; and most of these were probably pensioners. In agriculture, of course, there is still a good deal of seasonal and occasional employment open to such men. Although in metal manufacture there had been an increase of about 13 per cent in the total numbers employed, a steady decline had taken place in the numbers over 65; in fact, a large proportion of those who remained may have been merely ancillary labour. Much the same may be true for the chemical industries. The decline in the numbers over 65 in engineering and shipbuilding is confirmed by the Census Tables; these show a decline between 1951 and 1961 from about 3·0 to 2·3 per cent of all employed men.

It has been said that in the mid 'fifties the redundancies experienced in the cotton industry inclined a number of men over 65 to retire. While it is often expected that a contracting industry of this kind will tend to retain its older employees, in this case the introduction of new machines and of three-shift working in some mills would no doubt have had the opposite effect. The term 'Building' must be taken to include a certain amount of civil engineering and the building departments of local authorities, etc. A large proportion of the men over 65 in the industry are believed to be among those employed on maintenance and repair work; and the amount of this type of work seems to vary from 30 to 40 per cent of all building work (apart from civil engineering) in any single year. This, of course, has always tended to give the older man a fair chance of remaining on the job.

The contraction of labour on the railways was not apparently accompanied by any increase in the proportion over 65. Road motor transport, it must be noted, does not include the motor vehicles owned by manufacturing or commercial firms of all kinds; the figures do not, therefore, reflect the volume of motor transport as it has increased over the years. In the distributive trades the numbers over 65 have kept more or less level with the expansion in retailing, though for a time they seemed to show some proportionate growth. The overall figures must have run parallel with the increase in purchasing power. It is possible, however, that the rate of growth is now beginning to slow-down, as demand reaches a saturation point and as rationalisation begins to affect the retail trades; they may also be failing to retain young male labour.

Finally, there are the trends in employment over the last forty years. The Census has been taken every ten years (except for 1941); and we have to rely, of course, on the statements made by the men and women who have completed the forms. It must be here remembered that only since the late 'forties has the term 'retirement' come to have a more or less precise statutory connotation; and thus only since then would a man be likely to make a clean-cut distinction in his mind between employment and retirement. In earlier Census years many older men probably recorded themselves as still employed when they really meant that they considered that they were still available for employment. Table VII shows what percentages of the male population of later ages stated that they were at least still in the labour market, if anyone cared to employ them.

Table VII

APPROXIMATE PERCENTAGES OF OLDER MEN RECORDED AS BEING 'AT WORK' IN ENGLAND AND WALES IN THE CENSUS YEARS AND AGE GROUPS INDICATED

Year		*Age groups*	
	60–64	*65–69*	*70–74*
1921	88·7	79·5	52·6
1931	87·2	64·9	41·7
1951	87·5	47·2	27·3
1961	91·0	39·7	21·3

There are additional grounds (beyond the proviso I have already made) for suspecting that most or all of these figures are slightly inflated. Some of the chances of such a bias are inherent in the methods that have to be used in building up Census returns; the methods have not been uniform throughout, especially in regard to information about the occupations followed. In this matter the chances of error or of omission would almost certainly increase with the age of the informants. To take one factor alone, the older the age group with which we are dealing, the more limited and specialised the range of occupations its members claim to be following. For instance, at least 40 per cent of those still 'at work' in their early seventies described themselves in 1951 as professional men, administrators, farmers and clerical workers, or indicated that they were in some way employing the labour of others. Since descriptions of this kind are almost as much a matter of status as of livelihood, it would be difficult to say how far elderly persons are disposed to overlook the inquiry whether they are or are not 'retired'.

This, however, does not affect the broad trend embodied in the figures. If we have to be cautious with them, the bias is likely throughout to have been in the same upward direction.

It appears, then, that the country may be passing from a time when it was exceptional for men to be retired by their late sixties or even beyond, to a time when it will be exceptional for them *not* to be retired by that age. The age at which individuals must leave off working will never be so firmly established as the earliest age at which they can leave school and enter employment. But common practices could make it almost as inevitable; and many will find their post-employment phase as long as their period of childhood and schooling. In that case some adjustment will be needed in our social values.

But it is proper for us to take a very brief look at the *industrial setting* within which this human drama of the ages is slowly unfolding. What is happening in it has a direct bearing upon the policy of managements and the decision as to what constitutes an older man's continued employability.

3 *Industrial Setting for a Policy of Retirement*

We will now try to define the industrial changes that are taking place. Most economists seem at the moment to be thinking in terms of a time factor; they ask, for instance, how much capital equipment will have to be installed to raise the level of the national product by an annual average of 3 or 4 per cent. But in my own context the time factor is irrelevant. I simply take it that when a current of technological innovations gets under way, it will sooner or later affect every branch of industry. For me the question is not how long it will take but what social dilemmas it is likely to generate in its course.

Naturally the pace of industrial change could quicken under the stimulus of competition. For the matter of that, new methods of fabricating or processing products could merely become fashionable, provided the estimated gains seem to justify the costs of installation. On the other side, a human resistance to radical changes in the methods of production may take many forms; and the resistance is not always irrational. The rate at which new methods can be assimilated into an undertaking depends upon the effects they are likely to have on established patterns of forecasting, marketing and labour relations. The amount of the overall re-organisation that would be needed can only be gauged by men who are intimately concerned with the running of the firm. To begin with, we must admit that we are faced with a major change in our methods of production. The change will not penetrate all industries to the same extent or at an even pace; but none of them will remain unaffected. What has happened is this. A number of basic principles established in physics and chemistry (basic, at all events, as we now understand these sciences) have simultaneously 'worked loose', so to speak, into the applied sciences of engineering and machine design. They have become integrated with the economie forces of production. At the same time the social scientists who study the 'human factor' in industry believe that they have developed a set of principles governing such matters as labour deployment, the pace of operations and the most efficient man-machine relations. The applied principles of physics and chemistry need no immediate correction; they tell us all we want to know for the time being about directing power to the working parts of a machine, constructing automatic systems and dealing with the chemical changes in the materials handled. But the principles that govern man-machine relations do require a considerable amount of correction, for we are still largely ignorant of the ways in which men work and of the physical and mental consequences their work is likely to have for them.

Since people are nowadays quick to investigate any problem that has a human content, groups of physiologists and psychologists have been studying the applied science termed 'human engineering' in the U.S.A. and 'ergonomics' in our own country. Their aim in brief is to influence machine design and the planning of work rhythms, so that these can be made better fitted to man's inherent capacity. But all these last activities, significant as they are going to be for the human factor in industry, are still only of marginal importance in the technological revolution we are just entering. It must properly be thought of as a revolution, because a number of independent currents of research are beginning, as it were, to cross one another and to form in the process more and more complex patterns of technical application. If we examined each of these currents independently, we could of course trace its origins, as, for instance, in the industrial uses of electricity, in the design of self-regulating machines, or in the early invention of plastics, adhesives, etc. But what really matters is the very rapid 'cross-fertilisation' of so many specific lines of discovery in the field of mechanical production. Meanwhile the awareness among technologists of what can be turned to industrial uses is stimulating research workers to study afresh all the properties of natural substances; and their work is adding constantly to our industrial resources. If technologists do not yet govern our affairs, it is undeniable that they exercise a widening influence over social and educational policies.

There are two mistakes commonly made. The first is to imagine that there is nothing very novel in our situation, because most of the elements of which the technological revolution is composed did in fact exist in crude forms some years ago. This is to overlook the remarkable qualitative changes that can take place with the 'cross-fertilisation' of a large number of lines of research. The second mistake lies in concentrating too much attention upon 'automation'. Many industries, that are not immediately susceptible to automation, are also on the verge of revolutionary changes; and in most of them the changes will have the same effec of reducing or modifying the manpower needed for a given quantity of output. We shall be confronted in most of them with the same kind of social dilemma.

Automation, however, has become for many the typical form of the new-model industry; and it would be well to examine in passing what it means. Various definitions of it have, of course, been attempted. Thus, 'Automation is a means of analysing, organising and controlling production processes to achieve optimum use of all productive resources—mechanical and material as well as human'. Again, 'Automation is the technology of automatic working, in which the handling methods, the processes and the design of the processed materials are integrated to utilise as fully as is economically justifiable the mechanisation of thought and effort in order to achieve an automatic and in some cases a self-regulating chain of processes'.

Such definitions are well enough in their way; but they seem to me to refer only to the final outcome of all the basic factors that have suddenly combined to make automation possible.

These basic factors might perhaps be summarised in the following terms.

1. We are now able to convert many sources of energy into electrical currents, and to use them as an easily applied form of power in all manner of machine work.

2. Through systems of electronic components we can now initiate operations at speeds that are of a very different order from the speed of action we normally experience in our own organisms or in the natural world around us. Such almost incredible speeds of operation can nevertheless be intellectually measured and managed by the human mind.

3. Most important, we have come to recognise that many, and perhaps ultimately all, natural processes can be thought of as sequences or as convergent sequences of unitary stages, or again as composed of particles in motion. Though such processes appear to the observer to be continuous qualitative wholes, they can yet be expressed mathematically in quantitative terms. Natural substances, thus thought of and industrially processed, emerge at the end as new products that satisfy our every day needs. While that is to say, from the industrial standpoint the final product may have been assembled in unitary steps, it reaches us as a useful or an aesthetic commodity. Each of the unitary steps in the process can be made subject to electronic controls, whether as a 'flow' or through the automatic transfer of components from stage to stage. In times past, no doubt, man conceived natural and industrial processes as being too continuous to be broken down into a sequence of minute steps. Work demanded a large-scale manipulation by craftsmen or operatives.

4. Many such sequences can, of course, be combined into a vast variety of patterns, all under electronic controls; and these patterns are presumably capable of attaining a complexity that would be limited only by the stretch of man's mathematical imagination. That is the major distinctive characteristic of automation. It means that the coalescence of two streams of discovery—that of electronic speeds and that of the use of

unitary stages in production—has set free a sudden burst of inventive energy.

5. One result will be that of enhancing the industrial importance of design engineers and of the technicians who are responsible for constructing these automatic installations. Each component of an automated machine, and the machine itself, needs to be so thoroughly tested and made good, that in effect it is guaranteed to continue in operation with the minimum of repair. It is likely, moreover, that to an increasing extent, components will be made replaceable, so that machine faults can be rectified without retarding production. This of itself would not reduce the need for routine maintenance and inspection; but it would tend to concentrate such duties into the hands of a relatively few specialised technicians.

The principles underlying automation can already, as I say, be applied to many industrial processes; in fact, these principles are what gives the term its distinct meaning. In some branches of engineering automation is beginning to replace the human factor in the operations of, e.g. lifting, turning, clamping and rotating components between one act of shaping or assembly and the next. Its uses are especially obvious where the materials to be processed are fluids or can be reduced to particles of a standard consistency and thus be made to 'flow' like fluids. The earliest applications have been in such industries as oil refining, brick making, cement, paper making, glass, chemicals, baking and telecommunication. But there is no industry that will not in some measure and at varying rates come under its influence.

Automation, however, is only one of the ways in which technical changes are going to effect the deployment, and later also the selection, of labour. In mining, for example, and on the docks new and elaborate machinery is being installed; and this necessarily precedes the stage at which remote control of many operations can be envisaged. In the building industry we can foresee the increasing use of standard components and of pre-fabricated units; and in the printing industry new methods of production have been devised if not yet fully applied. Meanwhile, the gradual replacement for many purposes of natural materials by plastics and man-made fibres is lessening the need for labour employed on the inspection and refining of natural substances; again, the adoption of more efficient adhesives, varnishes, paints, etc., is modifying methods of production in a number of industries.

When a new industrial plant is being designed, the technological 'break-through' could be very rapid and complete. But limited ground space or inconvenient layout in an existing plant would often retard the application of new techniques. These delaying factors could, however, only be effective for a matter of a few years. Provided an industry can find the management and the trained labour it needs, its manufacturing plants will gradually be erected or re-designed. The potential pace set by technologists would then appear to be the pace normal for industrial progress. Though at present the rate at which management can assimilate technical innovations may be comparatively slow, the process will gather speed in the measure in which methods of building construction themselves become revolutionised.

We have now to see what are likely to be the *social* consequences of this overall revolution. By the time the change-over is fairly complete, the ways in which labour is deployed and the skills required will differ widely from those of an earlier and less sophisticated economy. To begin with, for *any given level* of output there would be far fewer operatives employed on process production or on the machining and assembly of components. Such men are still ordinarily classed as 'partly skilled'; but the term is, I think, already becoming very inappropriate. The degree of insight and reliability demanded of them is steadily increasing with the increasing complexity of installations.

Selection and training methods are almost certain to be more exacting and scientific, and the applied science of 'ergonomics' will probably have a good deal to say about the optimum number of shift hours a man should work on jobs of this kind.

It is usually assumed that the numbers of skilled maintenance workers in a plant would increase proportionately; whether their numbers would also increase absolutely for a given level of output, seems less clear. Indubitably the type and the range of skills needed are changing. But will industry require in the long run a much larger supply of skilled labour? Of course, if we measure the shortage of such labour by the degree of mobility shown in several industries among maintenance engineers and electricians, we are probably right in thinking that a larger supply of them could readily be absorbed; the rate of mobility of trained labour from one firm to another only begins to slow down when all the industrial firms of an area have attained a stable complement. But once an adequate amount of trained labour has been assured, other factors operate to limit the absolute numbers of maintenance men needed by an undertaking; for the intake of new trainees would no longer be conditioned simply by the level of turnover management finds it has to expect.

With modern installations it pays management to conserve rather than repair machinery. It may pay also to have all components replaceable, and to concentrate any major repairs that have to be effected in specialised central workshops. Routine inspection and testing would always be needed; but this can be left to specialists, who might in some instances be more conveniently laid on from the firms that originally supplied the machines. With smaller manufacturers that might indeed become the regular practice. There are in any case signs that such specialised technicians will become less of an old-style Trade Union than a conscious and incorporated professional body; and one is disposed to think that in the process supervisory functions will themselves be modified, especially if we also allow for the gradual upgrading of the responsibilities of production operatives.

In addition to the operative and maintenance staffs there is a third type of labour employed in industry. These are the men sometimes referred to as ancillary workers, i.e. factory and yard labourers, craftsmen's mates, cleaners, messengers and some unskilled labour at the points of delivery and despatch. They are of interest to us—first because some work of this kind is often committed to the older employees of a firm, and secondly because some economists appear to think that demand for this form of labour will gradually diminish.

Certainly much relatively unskilled work, such as that involved in the humping and moving of materials or the packing and despatch of products, can be integrated into a sequence of mechanised processes. Moreover, machines could in some instances be used in place of the simple manual work needed for sweeping and allied jobs; and in that case a modicum of skill, strength and judgment would often be required. But the number of workers with a minimum of training that a firm is prepared to employ depends in reality upon an important factor, that is sometimes overlooked, i.e. upon the range of amenities an employer thinks proper to lay on in the plant. Such industrial amenities can be very varied—from canteens, recreation rooms, cloak rooms and clinics to gardens, parking spaces and sports grounds. These would all need a proportion of lower grade labour; and if services of this kind were to increase inside the industrial ambit, the number of 'unskilled' jobs would increase proportionately.

I find it impossible, however, to predict at present how far it will be within the industries themselves (or perhaps financed directly by the industries) that these varied services and amenities expand. We may be sure that at the national level the welfare services will develop continuously, together with facilities for recreation and sport; and in that case there will still be room in these fields for some relatively unskilled and older labour. But they may become steadily less important in both manufacturing and non-manufacturing industries.

Thus in the long run there are bound to be changes in the industrial functions of most employed men; and these changes, as they come about, will gradually affect, for instance, both the selection *in* and the selection *out* of operatives. Together with the policy of enlarging the duties of a fully trained operative would go a plan for building into his industrial career some kind of a promotion ladder. Though this may not yet be the practice in all automatic or semi-automatic industries, industrial policy is evidently moving in that direction. In effect, the operative man-power needed would be recruited into the labouring grades; and a man's promotion would come with his proven aptitude and growing experience.

Men initiated and trained in this way (e.g. for mining, civil engineering and dock operations, or in the chemical, metal and power generating industries) would usually be capable of mastering a wide range of machine processes or of becoming familiar with large installations. It would be inappropriate to call such men 'semi-skilled' in the sense in which the term is applied to a man trained for repetitive work on an individual machine.

But it must be pointed out that the adoption of some kind of promotion ladder on the factory floor only tends to strengthen an employer's preference for a rigid age of retirement. His argument is that a system of promotions cannot be made to work smoothly, unless the age at which all his employees withdraw from the labour force is pre-determined. His obvious solution is to clear the field at about the age at which men become pensionable. For that is assumed to be the age at which many of them are in any case prepared to leave their normal jobs. This is by no means the only reason for adopting a retiring age; but I mention it because I think it is one that has been overlooked. It means in effect, that a policy long accepted in some branches of clerical and professional employment is now extending to a number of manual workers.

What then, have we to pay, humanly speaking, for a technical revolution of these dimensions? There are probably at least four consequences that we can identify; and they will all need social adjustments.

1. At varying stages of their working lives large numbers of men will have to move from one industry or one job to another. That will involve processes of re-training and re-settlement; and its implications, as I said earlier, will not be further discussed here.

2. We have also to ask ourselves what industries will offer a stable and growing market for labour. No doubt new industries will emerge as others contract. It is by no means certain, however, that the products (or the services) of an emergent industry will not be to some extent replacing those of some established industry and so lead to still further contractions. Consumption is not invariably elastic or cumulative. Provided the basic manufacturing industries remain buoyant, the most permanently useful fields of expanding employment will probably lie in services and in constructional work. Some of this will find its own level, as, e.g. in retailing, the tourist trade, sports and entertainments; but much of it as in the Health and Social Services or in road making will need administrative diversions of an appropriate proportion of the national income.

We could expect some statistical evidence of a gradual movement of labour into such services, as purchasing power begins to rise in the community. This has already been suggested as true for the distributive trades. (See Table VI.) The Ministry of Labour annual Tables show a recent increase in male employment where we might have looked for it.[1]

These figures must not be taken as too precise, especially as they were based on a 1 per cent sample. Methods of classification are also likely to have changed a little, not least in the last category, which includes a diversity of more or less commercial services. I add for reference a parallel Table showing the

[1] *Ministry of Labour Gazette*, June 1952, 1958 and 1965.

numbers of men so employed aged 65 and over in the same years.

Table VIII

NUMBERS OF MEN (IN THOUSANDS) EMPLOYED IN VARIOUS SERVICES IN THE YEARS INDICATED

Industry	*Numbers of Men Employed* (in thousands)		
	1950	*1957*	*1964*
Motor repairs and garages	218	269	336
Theatres, cinemas, etc.	62	60	72
Sports, betting, etc.	46	39	63
Catering, hotels, etc.	187	179	218
Various welfare, charitable, cleansing and other services	50	54	154

Table IX

NUMBERS OF MEN AGED 65 AND OVER (IN THOUSANDS) EMPLOYED IN VARIOUS SERVICES IN THE YEARS INDICATED

Industry	*Numbers of Men of 65+ Employed* (in thousands)		
	1951	*1957*	*1964*
Motor repairs and garages	7	8	12
Theatres, cinemas, etc.	4	5	4
Sports, betting, etc.	3	6	8
Catering, hotels, etc.	14	18	19
Various welfare, charitable, cleansing, and other services	2	4	8

There has apparently been a gratifying rise in the numbers of older men in these services; and to some extent the rise has been proportionate. Since the numbers should include part-time workers, this may indicate where a few retired men are finding their way. But we cannot be sure that the trend will continue.

3. It is probable that in a good many industries the process of selecting operatives will become more scientific. This is not a matter of passing them through medical or psychological tests; the medical examination of applicants need go no further than it does already in several undertakings. But there are two

new elements emerging. First is the fact that operatives are being more systematically trained for their varied duties in an industrial unit; and secondly, management will be trying to enlarge its responsibilities in such fields as that of the judicious selection and training of the right men for the jobs, as it finds its powers of decision progressively circumscribed by the use of computors in forecasting output and market trends.

4. But the most important of the social consequences is likely to be that affecting the close of the working life. If we are going to have a shorter working week and an increase in communal 'leisure', it does not necessarily follow that the additional free hours will be evenly distributed. It is recognised, for instance, that many younger men are inclined to use their free hours simply to seek supplementary jobs, mostly on a part-time basis. The problem is to know whether in so doing they are in reality competing for part-time or casual work, that might otherwise have been filled by competent men in their late sixties. In that case, though the aggregate amount of 'leisure' increases in the community, the result would only be to concentrate an undue and an unwelcome proportion of it into the later years of a man's life. Thus not only is there, as we have seen, a growing tendency to terminate the normal working life at an arbitrary age; the market for part-time and casual jobs might also be largely occupied by younger men, who could no doubt often out-bid their older rivals. We can assume, in short, that whatever technical changes take place in manufacture, there will continue to be a substantial market for more or less unskilled casual labour; and the pay packet it offers has, we must admit, some attraction for young men and for those with growing families.

I have been looking in this chapter mainly at the large-scale tide of industrial changes, as they affect in particular the prospects of the older men. But what I have said does not explain precisely how such men come to be individually 'selected out' from their normal jobs, by reason of their age or some other debilitating condition. To understand that we have to go to the factory floor or the building site, where transactions of the kind are effected from day to day. The nature of the decisions made about a man's continued employability, and the principles that govern these decisions, have never been studied as intimately as they deserve. It is almost taken for granted that they are in many cases arbitrary and unsystematic.

4 *The Ultimate Test of an Older Man's Employability*

Men at work are usually deployed in departmental teams; and it follows that each member of such a team must be capable of a minimum standard of performance. At all events he must not fall too far below an acceptable level. The standard might, of course, have been set by the findings of a Work Study enquiry; or it might be (and often, I think, is) set simply by conventional ideas in the minds of supervisors. Any men whose performances fall permanently below that standard range would be judged to have become 'marginal' labour. If they are still retained in their departments, it is either because of a serious labour shortage or because employers are unwilling to discharge long service men until they can at least claim a pension.

The members of supervisory staffs deploy the labour committed to them on factory floor, building site or dock; and the extent to which they can continue to utilise 'sub-standard' labour is the real limiting factor that we have to allow for. The extent to which they can do so is measured in turn by the degree to which labour costs would be raised or output retarded by the presence of older men. The strange thing is that this elementary aspect of the 'ageing' problem has been almost entirely overlooked. There are reasons for that neglect. What happens in a department does not always come to the attention of higher management; and consequently detailed records may not be kept. Overall directives may have been conveyed to a supervisor; and he would then be left to interpret them as best he could. Again the need to re-deploy labour from time to time is more or less taken for granted by supervisors. The process of selecting or of 'shelving' individual employees goes on over so protracted a period of months or years, that it is rarely given serious objective thought. Only where the dilution of standard labour with 'marginal' workers seems to a supervisor to be taxing too far his powers of adjustment will he make representations to higher management.

On this subject the scanty literature that deals with industrial supervision is of little use. It is concerned with organisational problems that are no doubt relevant; but it tells us almost nothing about the job of deploying teams of men of very diverse ages, states of health and innate aptitudes.

On the other hand, industrial psychologists, when they inquire into the problem, usually start off by taking a sample of ageing or of partially disabled employees, and then go on to consider what types of work might in theory be still suitable for them. They do not necessarily ask whether the jobs they recommend would be available; and if they do discuss the problem with supervisors, they tend to frame their questions in general terms—the kinds of question that are calculated to elicit only abstract and conventional responses. We ought now to reverse the whole method and, taking the work situation as we find it, inquire of supervisors what *proportions* of 'marginal' men they can safely utilise without the risk of retarding output or raising costs. For that must always be the ultimate test of a worker's continued employability for any given job.

It has been recognised for some time that, once employees are past 55 or 60, a steadily increasing proportion of them must in fact be moved to less exacting work; and the process is usually a matter of negotiation between a man and his supervisor. Now, if it so happens that the availability of such light jobs in a department is diminishing, the problem of re-deploying the older men can easily become embarrassing; and this is one of the elements that is today commending to employers the policy of a rigid retiring age. To make the problem clear, I will examine the concrete evidence from a few highly mechanised industries. The mistake committed by social theorists is to imagine that age in years has little influence on a man's working capacity whereas for supervisors it is often in practice the crucial test.

An attempt was made to summarise the state of affairs (1961) in an engineering firm in the Home Counties, that employed in its Works somewhat more than 2000 male manual workers.[1] The proportion aged 55–64 was unusually high—over 20 per cent; this must have been due to the stage reached in the life of the firm and its relative success in retaining labour. It accounts in part for an adherence to the policy of retiring all men at 65. Medical records and the evidence of supervisors were used to identify which men were 'sub-standard' as measured by normal performance. In a few instances, especially among the younger men, the condition may have been only temporary.

This was known to be a very tolerant firm. 'It would appear that by the time the early fifties are reached a percentage of workmen are receiving preferential treatment. . . . I think that the supervisor is solving this type of work problem as a normal task, and hardly appreciating the extent of it. Allowances are made for the men by dropping targets to an acceptable level or by reserving for them jobs where the pressure is lower.'

Much of the work involved the shaping, fabricating, welding, surfacing and packing of batches of heavy or fairly heavy components. In several of the departments a high tempo could be attained. The welding department was one of these. A rhythm of sustained effort was demanded in placing the bars against electrodes, removing surplus metal with automatic chisels and trimming with abrasive disks. Only on a few of the welding operations could room be found for comparatively unfit men. About 6 per cent of the employees of the department were older men of the type recognised to be 'sub-standard'. Surfacing (i.e. the operation of a galvanizing bath) could accommodate about the same proportion of the less fit older men; but these were mostly on ancillary jobs outside the surfacing units. Packing was admitted to be heavy work; and sub-standard men accounted for little more than 3 per cent of those in the packing department.

[1] Private communication.

On the other hand, there was less difficulty experienced in re-deploying 'marginal' labour in the maintenance and stores departments. About 12 per cent on maintenance were older men of the type that could no longer be expected to make the full grade. There was a good deal of work in the department where pace was of little importance; and the definition can be stretched to include such jobs as the issue of maintenance stores. In the main stores at least half the labour was composed of men in a similar physical condition; much of their work was that of helping to check the quantities and qualities of materials, examine components on delivery, issue small accessories etc.

It must not be assumed that supervisors could have gone no further in utilising 'marginal' men; but it seems likely from the description that they were coming somewhere near saturation point. A considerable number of the older men were, of course, thoroughly effective. Those less than effective were reaching proportions that could probably not have been increased without an undue rise in labour costs on each unit of production.

An inquiry carried out in a plant manufacturing domestic furniture (1956) also had been based largely on the judgements of supervisors.[1] It concentrated upon the effectiveness of men from 55 upwards—mainly because it had been surmised that the problem would here become significant. The male labour force was one of approximately 2000, some 12 per cent of it in the older age range. At the time the firm had no ruling about retirement; and there were consequently a number of employees over 65. Production methods were, for that industry, at an advanced stage of mechanisation. Allowing for the difference of the materials used, it had some resemblance to engineering, —a fact of which the industry is conscious. It affected in much the same way the amount of flexibility a supervisor could show in trying to accommodate 'sub-standard' men. Though the report was mainly concerned with the physical condition of

[1] *Ageing on the Factory Floor*. The Nuffield Foundation 1957.

individual men and with the transitions they had made, the complementary role of supervision was given almost as much space. It was evident that the problem became more acute once men were passing into their sixties. Industrial and medical records showed that not more than 10 per cent of the men in their late fifties had apparently been moved to lighter operations, though it seemed clear in several cases that even by that age the transfer had become permanent. But it also appeared, states the report, that 'at a liberal estimate somewhere about three in ten of the men in their early sixties were permanently incapacitated for full normal duty; and in the case of several others some allowances had to be made'.

If there is any contradiction between this assessment and that made above in an engineering plant, it may be a matter of medical or industrial definitions. But it is more likely to reside in the average levels of effort demanded in the two industries. 'The records suggest that in road transport, for example, or under factory conditions that demand pace and continuity on shift work the incidence of such transfers and adjustments would become noticeable at an earlier average age than in furniture production. . . . A careful comparison of the varied working conditions to which men are subjected will probably reveal as varied a pattern in the occupational experiences of the ageing'. The report, however, hints that changes in the furniture industry were imminent. 'It is the element of co-ordinated overall timing in production that is decisive. Under modern factory conditions it is becoming necessary to select men who can maintain the overall continuity; and as far as ageing men are concerned, it becomes a matter of sorting out what operations they can still perform without impeding the flow of production. So far as the breakdown of operations is reaching its limits and may now be replaced by a new cycle of co-ordinated and combined operations, shop supervisors and foremen are likely to find fewer of the relatively light operations to which older men have been customarily transferred'.

While it is never possible to say precisely what latitude

supervisors might have for re-adjusting jobs, the impression in this case was that several of them had about stretched ingenuity to the limit. Some 4 per cent of manual employees were over 65; and it was clear that at least 60 per cent of these had been placed on modified or preferential work. A good many of them were light labourers; and some who had acquired skill in the use of hand tools could be relegated to the job of repairing and making good parts as they left the machine shop. In furniture production the continued employability of ailing or ageing men seemed to depend on the answer to two main questions: i.e. how far are shop supervisors able to break down and reorganise operations in the interest of such men, and what reserves of skill and adaptability have the men themselves? The aim is always to have parts and sub-units moving along the flow as expeditiously as possible. The upshot is that a supervisor would assume that there is only a limited range of operations on which such men could safely be employed; and in consequence he is himself controlled by the practical extent to which he can break down the work of his department without increasing the labour force beyond an economic level.

A study that had been carried out by Mrs K. Wintringham, in the manufacturing town of Slough was based primarily on interviews with several hundred male manual workers.[1] They were all aged 55 and upwards. The survey included discussions about these same men with members of the supervisory staffs. Twenty-four establishments were visited, embracing chemicals, engineering, textiles, food processing, paper, etc. All available men within the age range selected were interviewed; and where possible their medical records were scrutinised.

The supervisors were not asked in this case how they managed to deal with such of the men as had become 'sub-standard' in performance; they were asked at what levels they

[1] *Workers Nearing Retirement*. Edited by Dr Alastair Heron and F. Le Gros Clark. The Nuffield Foundation 1963.

assessed their individual capacity for work. The impression they conveyed was one of tolerance. More than a fifth of the employees interviewed were over the pensionable age; and it was evident that these were physically a 'selected' group. The whole number whose capabilities were discussed with supervisors was 535 (507 of these had been personally interviewed). In broad terms, 41 per cent of the men of 55–64 were rated as at least 'satisfactory' or 'adequate', and 7 per cent as 'poor'; the remainder were considered 'eminently good'. The assessments of those who were over the pensionable age fell into much the same pattern; only 8 per cent of them were reckoned 'poor'.

The report comments, 'The industrial contribution made by these older men depended in great part on the care that had been taken in placing them on appropriate jobs. The older manual workers seemed rarely to have been retained solely in recognition of their past services, at all events beyond a pensionable age. This is the reason why less than 10 per cent of them were rated as poor propositions in either of the age groups. If they were really ineffective, they were retired'. The essence of it seemed to be that foremen had often helped to initiate moves to more or less appropriate jobs and consequently felt bound to claim that the men were at least 'adequate' for the work. They would try to transfer an older man before he reached the point of a breakdown; and there was frequently competition among foremen for openings that became available outside their own departments.

There are nevertheless grounds for thinking that in technically advanced industries management will be more and more compelled to deal with its 'marginal' labour by means of departments for scrap disposal and recovery, light stores, etc. A Merseyside industrial survey[1] though it did not examine supervisors about their individual employees, observed that the alternative work

[1] *Ageing and the Semi-skilled: A Survey in Manufacturing Industry on Merseyside*. Dr Alastiar Heron and Dr Sheila M. Chown. Medical Research Council. H.M.S.O. 1961.

available for an older man almost always involved change to a relatively menial occupation, with a loss of status and usually of earnings. In Slough, too, where a foreman went so far as to state that he preferred older men, he was usually commenting on those who were doing jobs that younger men disliked; it was felt that men who were contented with such jobs were hard to come by.

As a matter of fact, in the Slough firms a fairly large proportion of the older men must have been moved to jobs that needed a minimum of speed or skill. Almost 40 per cent of those in their early sixties were on such work as clearing scrap, sweeping, gardening, labouring in the stores, etc.; the proportion in the late sixties was much the same. Experience, of course, varied from firm to firm. But supervisors appeared to have adopted a uniform approach in the handling of such transfers. They usually wished to retain in their own departments a man for whom they had a liking; and they would therefore prepare his mind gradually for a move, so that it could be effected as soon as an opening offered.

A study had also been made (1954) of the experience of building foremen in selecting and deploying their less effective labour.[1] The report was based on communications from 78 building managers and foremen; in most cases the managers seem to have consulted their foremen before giving replies. The industry has, of course, several distinctive characteristics. In factory work materials and products pass from department to department, whereas on a building site new types of labour are drafted on to production as the work proceeds. If older and slower labour could be brought on only for clearing up and making good at the close of a contract, many foremen would be quite satisfied. A further point, of course, is that a large proportion of the national building labour force is permanently

[1] *Ageing Men in the Labour Force*. The problems of Organising Older Workers in the Building Industry. The Nuffield Foundation. 1955.

employed on repairs and maintenance work; the report estimates that at least a third of the man-power of the industry was then on jobs of that nature, where quality and reliability are usually more important than speed.

An attempt was made to arrive at some kind of estimate of the numbers of patently ageing men a foreman could handle. The replies depended upon the type of contract. So far as some of the foremen clearly had high-class or specialised work in mind, a limit of 20 per cent or so of elderly craftsmen was not considered unreasonable; but they often qualified their answers by contrasting the much lower proportion that would have been practicable on 'cheap' building work or in a casual labour force. In fact, a distinction was almost invariably made by the more discriminating foremen between one job and another. For instance, firms undertaking extensive civil engineering or demolition work would not allow of an average of more than 3 to 4 per cent of physically ageing men. One firm would have gone as high as 5 per cent for craftsmen, but not more than 2·5 per cent for labourers. On maintenance and some alteration work the proportion could plainly be much higher; the average lay between 15 and 20 per cent. But as far as the small building contracts were concerned, the estimates were fairly uniform; they mostly ranged between 5 and 10 per cent. A plastering specialist considered that a ratio of one in ten should not be exceeded; 'the ageing man would not in general stand the pace set by the young'.

On the whole foremen seem to prefer to have a few older men about them on the job; but they were still cautious in their estimates. They were often thinking of the comparative strains imposed on labourers servicing the craftsmen; the usual opinion was that brick two-storey houses presented less difficulty in this respect than multi-storey flats. For the ordinary run of building foremen, it may be said, much beyond 10 per cent of older men would have begun to tax their organising powers; but a maintenance foreman could usually manage with anything up to double the proportion possible on constructional work. It must be remembered that in building operations much depends on the hazards, obstacles and broken ground that are likely to be encountered; and it was plainly on these, as well as on the factor of costs, that a foreman had his mind. It was noticeable that a number of foremen tended to place the slower labourers on the more static jobs, e.g. the levelling of ground, trowelling of concrete, pipe laying and (if demolition work was in progress) the cleaning and stacking of bricks. One foreman remarked that he found the older men preferred rather to dig than to wheel a barrow, feed a mixer and not drive it; labouring for tradesmen, loading and unloading had little favour with them.

If we are to express the whole problem in abstract terms, it is sufficient to say that each mode of production settles more or less impersonally what mean level of physical and mental fitness is demanded of its human components. Invariably there are limits beyond which supervisors are not prepared to go by way of diluting their labour with men who fall below that standard. Such limits are not necessarily explicit in their minds; but they do enter into their daily reckonings.

I have had in this chapter to draw upon evidence from industries that were only at a stage of fairly advanced mechanisation. With the new techniques of production, supervisors are likely to have far less latitude in reorganising the labour of a department for the benefit of a few older men. Moreover the physical symptoms from which they can decide that it is time for a change of job will gradually become more elusive, as the work load shifts from a man's muscles to his mental apparatus.

While the organised relations of a factory department, a building site or a colliery are thus no doubt the ultimate test, these relations have all the time to adapt themselves to the conditions of a rapidly changing industry. Before we go further, it would be as well to see what are the wider economic forces that tend to control the thoughts and actions of supervisors and operatives alike.

5 *Economic Pressures Round the Close of the Working Life*

The rate of industrial change is now settled mainly by the interplay between management and organised labour. Even when the rate seems to slow down, the breathing spaces afforded by that interplay are not necessarily a bad thing; they represent the natural time taken for the minds of men to accommodate themselves collectively to each new balance of economic forces. I am now asking why a retiring age of any kind should so often be included (and that by mutual agreement) in a man's contract of service. Is it part of the cost we have to pay for accelerating the *tempo* of economic change?

Of course, once a Government has decided the age at which all men shall be *entitled* to a State pension, that age begins almost invariably to exert some influence on industrial policy. Parliament itself recognises no 'normal' retiring age (except in the case of its own employees)—only the legal minimum age of entitlement. But both sides of industry incline to see 65 as in some mysterious way a critical age; and that, after all, is not really surprising. When a new Pension Act was being debated in the 'twenties, some employers and certainly many trade unionists were among the political 'pressure groups' that helped to shape its terms. The age of entitlement had previously been 70; and 65 had begun to seem, not merely more equitable, but in times of unemployment much more convenient. Since the 'twenties the chances have always been that, whenever industrial negotiations touch upon the question of a mandatory retiring age, the age of 65 would be the first considered. There may be nothing to choose *biologically* between 65 and 67 or 63. But the human mind needs some elementary point of departure; and if 70 is plainly too late and 60 too early, a halfway stage is the simplest solution. We will only examine some of the more important of the economic factors that have been at work.

We have reached a time in our industrial history, at which one of the oldest demands of organised labour is at last coming to the surface; it had been for many years submerged under the shifting state of the economy. This demand springs from the natural urge among manual workers to secure some guaranteed continuity of employment. It had always been one of the more enduring purposes of the Trade Unions. But it was for long held in suspension, as it were, by the fact that their efforts were mainly concentrated upon wage levels and the hours and conditions of work. Moreover, the alternation of trade depressions and revivals, that characterised the hundred years down to 1940, seemed to them as much beyond the control of employers, as it was beyond that of labour; it made impracticable any demand for security on the job.

It is usually the men in middle life who dominate the floor at Union branches and conferences; and for them security of tenure on the job is obviously a matter of some domestic importance. A change in the pensionable age from 70 to 65 seemed to them both a humane measure and an insurance against their own futures. But there was more in their minds than that. The lower the age of the statutory pension, the easier would it be in times of unemployment to plead that all available jobs should be reserved for the men with growing families.

An industrial and social philosophy of this kind influence the thoughts of many men in the depressed 'thirties and a number of these are themselves now growing old. They have tended to accept the idea of some predestined age of withdrawal. Few manual workers seem now disposed to question the propriety of a fixed retiring age—at all events when it has been for some years the policy of their firm. Meanwhile, we are now in a phase of relatively full employment; and that, though it changes the emphasis a little, has not yet affected the basic philosophy. With fluctuations of trade in one industry or another the demand for a guaranteed security on the job is taking more definite forms. Thus there is, of course, the proposal for compensatory payments to meet redundancy; and to this is added on occasion the suggestion that in a falling market overtime work should be temporarily suspended or that the available work should be spread evenly over a firm's employees. On the other hand, a local shortage of labour will usually persuade employers—and especially those in medium-size firms—to relax temporarily, any ruling or custom they had adopted of retiring men at a pensionable age; they will be prepared to consider taking on a few men in their fifties or even beyond. But this is never likely to have more than a marginal effect upon the employment prospects of an older man once he had withdrawn completely from his normal job.

The admission by some employers that a demand for security of work is not unjustified has involved both parties in periods of negotiation. The course of discussion has rarely been made clear; but it does affect among other matters the question of retirement. There seems, for example, an inclination in several industries to suspend a long-established principle of seniority or 'first in, last out'. At any rate, Unions are apparently willing to concede, in exchange for other advantages, that the industrial grading of employees on merit shall override mere length of service. Again, it may be agreed in a firm that, where a compulsory age of retirement had already been recognised, the age at which an industrial superannuation can be claimed might be pre-dated by four or five years; for such a ruling may persuade a man who is patently ageing to take his superannuation and look for a job elsewhere. These arrangements make it more practicable, when any redundancy is threatened, to clear the field of some of the elderly and in many cases least effective men.

When changes in methods, or large-scale contractions in a whole industry, are sure to result in heavy redundancies, the problem can only be dealt with in a comprehensive manner. In coal mining, for example, one of the immediate solutions was to retire all the men who were entitled to draw a State pension. Mining had formerly been among the industries least affected nationally by any policy of rigid retirement; and what has happened with coal may be a warning that we must expect similar changes elsewhere.

But even when a firm goes no further than to plan some reorganisation or amalagamation such a process may be almost as disturbing as an overall contraction. Departments of a plant may be reduced in size; or the factory may become more specialized in its products. Though business as a whole may be expanding, the design of a new factory at some distance from the old site will often give a firm the chance of rationalising output and concentrating some of its labour force. In other words, it is not only the overall contraction of an industry that threatened security of employment; every technical innovation could nowadays have the same effect.

We will examine briefly another factor, that has probably been helping to shape managerial policy. In theory it might have only temporary consequences; but they are hard to predict. A number of manufacturing concerns expanded during and after the 1914–18 war; and in so doing they would, of course, have built up a relatively young labour force. The amount of labour turnover they experienced was variable. But at that time labour seems to have been comparatively stable; and many firms have retained with them a large proportion of their employees. The net result, thirty to forty years later, is that such firms are finding that an undue proportion of their long service men are growing too old at the same time; the age structure, in short, is becoming unbalanced.

The truth is that the rhythms of industrial development in the present century have had the effect of bringing this dilemma into unusual prominence. The problem is by no means universal; it may only affect single firms or single departments of a firm. But it seems sufficiently common to influence managerial calculations. Moreover, the impression it leaves is liable nowadays to be intensified by other considerations. Since the last war we have been systematically informed by the Government that our population is demonstrably 'ageing'; and though the demographic trends were then exaggerated, they would certainly have suggested to employers the importance of attracting into an industry its fair share of young labour. Techniques were already changing; and a man's long experience on a job, however valuable in itself, was liable to become an outmoded asset. It should now be the business of industrial statisticians to interpret to their employers the implications of the age structure of a firm's labour force; and at the same time they should be able to forecast the quantity and quality of the man-power it will require in the future. Their estimates are a precaution against the risk that the intake of young and trainable labour might remain at too low a level. In a way the problem is not unlike that presented by the 'block' of promotion in a large office. But it must be noted that these demographic fluctuations will often exert a two-sided influence on managerial policy. When it appears probable that a shortage of young labour is developing in an area, managers are anxious to maintain a steady rate of recruitment; they might otherwise acquire a local reputation of offering a poor employment prospect. On the other hand, when there is a local 'bulge' of school-leavers to be absorbed, the Ministry impresses on employers the need to take their fair share. In either case we must realise that it would be imperative to maintain a steady flow of older employees out of the labour force; and that is most effectively achieved through the adoption of some kind of retiring age. The urge to secure young recruits may well override an inclination to conserve the elements of reliability felt to be embodied in a number of the older employees.

When we speak of promotion, it should be noted that there are signs that schemes of promotion are being applied more

generally to manual workers as well as to staff employees. This is a matter already referred to (Chapter 3); and I want to enlarge upon it a little further. Some undertakings have introduced methods for upgrading operatives by merit and experience; and such promotions, however unsubstantial they may be in some respects, would usually carry an addition to the pay packet. The grades in any working team are frequently given specific names; and they do impart to the team a structural quality it may formerly have lacked.

There are several advantages to be gained by management from an upgrading system. It reflects the changes that are going on both here and in the U.S.A. in industrial training methods and in the functions of operatives. Mr S. Barkin referred to these changes in the paper from which I quoted earlier.[1] 'An operative's introduction to the new jobs is not by way of a long apprenticeship on a machine. Rather, is it derived from his ability to perceive relationships among jobs and operations . . . to assume the responsibilities inherent in the job. These new occupations, which are multiplying throughout the economy, place a premium not on the man who takes orders but on the man who responsibly supervises a machine or process'. For another thing, it is felt by employers that the mere fact that some type of promotion ladder has been built into an industrial department is more likely to attract labour of the right quality.

But of course all this can have exactly the same effect for an older operative as it would have in an administrative department. In neither case must promotion be unduly 'blocked'; there is, moreover, something aesthetically appealing about the notion of a definable working life, within the limits of which any operative has a fair chance of showing how far he has been able to profit from his training and experience.

But when a firm is led by some argument to adopt a super-

[1] S. Barkin, *Fitting Jobs to the Unemployed Older Persons*, U.S.A., 1961.

annuation scheme, it usually wants to avoid any appearance of discrimination. A Trade Union might object that one man is retained beyond his pensionable age, while another has been unwillingly retired. Again, the whole process has been rationalised into the humane principle that, since a man must be retired sooner or later, it is better for him to know in advance the precise date of the event; a foreknowledge ought to mitigate the moods of anxiety engendered in a man who is growing conscious of his age. Though the choice of a superannuable age must always be arbitrary, it enables an employer to escape from these dilemmas; and he probably has a taste in any case for simple administrative book-keeping. Certainly his Insurance Company has. Where a *private individual* takes out an Endowment Policy, it is preferable to close the account the moment he reaches the prescribed age; and there is little distinction, after all, when a firm insures a whole group of employees. Ordinarily the motives that lead an employer to take out a group insurance of this kind are associated in his mind with a uniform age, which may or may not be the exact age of 65; he is impressed by the arguments for fairness and equity. But if at a later stage he sees good reason for modifying the scheme into a more flexible form, he usually has to meet some resistance from his Accounts Department. A superannuation scheme, that might in theory have been in the first instance cast into a relatively flexible form, cannot so readily be re-designed once the actuarial and preparatory book-keeping work has been completed. This disposes in some measure of the commonly held belief that there are legal barriers to a flexible scheme of industrial superannuation. There may be legal difficulties about the official approval of a scheme, but they are not insuperable, and changes in the Law may well make for wider flexibility.

The impact made by all such arguments on both sides of industry has been strengthened by the general impression that the pace of work is beginning to shorten the average period of

effective service. In other words, men are thought to be showing their age a year or two earlier than they need have done under less exacting conditions. There is not much statistical evidence to support this theory; but that does not necessarily mean that it has no foundation. In any case innovations must always result in some wastage among the older employees. A few of them, even if they had been acclimatised to the old conditions, fail to make the grade. What apparently happens is that the additional effort demanded in mastering unfamiliar methods may precipitate a latent sense of insufficiency. The proportions that fail to make the grade to a new job probably depend both on the relative ages of the men and on the training methods adopted, as well as on the degree of versatility shown by the men themselves.

When wastage occurs among the older operatives of a firm for this or any other cause (except chronic invalidity), the problem often arises of what to do with them until they become pensionable. For as we have already seen (Chapter 4), some marginal wastage is likely to take place among men in their early sixties or even before. Indeed, the very fact that it overtakes some men before they have become pensionable only serves to strengthen the argument for a mandatory age of final withdrawal; otherwise the numbers to be placed on preferential tasks might grow inconveniently large. At this point we come back immediately to the intimate relations prevailing on a shop floor or a building site. Here the pace and the continuity of output expected would normally be measured by the capacities shown by an able-bodied worker. If alternative jobs have to be found for a few older employees, it is primarily the concern of supervisors and foremen; and it may subsequently have to be made the concern of higher management.

We really do come now to the heart of the matter. There may be no question to-day of letting an operative go too far in moderating his normal effort or falling completely out of rhythm with the working team of which he forms part. But surely, if he is willing and still vigorous enough, he could be moved to some alternative job where the strain is less pronounced.

So central has become this problem of *alternative work*, that I must examine it in some detail. It is more complicated than might appear, because it can, for instance, involve competing claims for a very limited and occasionally a diminishing supply of light jobs. Such a survey will give us a chance to look into one of the obscurer and less familiar departments of modern industry.

6 *The Assumption that Alternative Jobs must be Available*

(1) *In Manufacturing Industries*

So far I have mainly discussed the extent to which 'sub-standard' men can still be assimilated into the *normal work of a department.* But it is recognised that there still survive in industry a number of the specific jobs that are always referred to as appropriate *light* or *alternative work.* Many such jobs have the advantage of being isolated from the organised rhythms of production.

Thus the Director General of the International Labour Office, dealing with the whole subject of age in his 1962 Report,[1] states that, 'In some countries certain types of employment are set aside for older workers of advanced years or such workers are given preference in respect of them. This is the case in France (for watchmen, cleaners, liftmen); and in Sweden municipalities often follow this practice with regard to older persons no longer able to compete on an equal footing with younger workers'. In 1953 the Ministry of Labour's National Advisory Committee on the Employment of Older Men and Women plainly had the same method in mind.[2] 'All men and women employed in industry, commerce, the professions or elsewhere, who can give effective service, either in their normal work or *any alternative work which their employers can make available,* should be given the opportunity without regard to age to continue at work if they so wish'. Their Second Report in 1955 was more precise[3]—'There is . . . scope for the development of schemes for the employment of people of

[1] International Labour Conference. Report 1 (Part 1). Report of the Director General. *Older People—Work and Retirement.* International Labour Office, Geneva. 1962.

[2] London, H.M.S.O., 1953 [3] London, H.M.S.O., 1955.

pensionable age on part-time jobs requiring no special skill; for example, messengers and handymen, office boys and school traffic wardens. It seems that where schemes of this kind have been introduced they have proved popular and there have been more applicants than jobs available'.

It appears to me that most manufacturing firms retain at least some of these jobs under their traditional names; and after reflection managers can usually grade as 'relatively light' several other forms of unskilled labouring work. Such industries as transport and coal mining reserve for the purpose a number of *transfer jobs*, that are in many instances peculiar to themselves. But manufacturing plants are as a whole still fairly uniform in their practice, though they vary widely in detail. As a preliminary step, information was sought on the subject from 34 manufacturing concerns, all at an advanced stage of technical development. They probably represent the range of variations one would encounter in plants at a similar phase of mechanisation. The firms approached included: Metal Manufacture (4), General Engineering (5), Motor Manufacture (2), Chemicals (5), Glass and Rubber (3), Oil Refineries (1), Food Processing, Oils and Fats (8), Clothing (2), and a miscellaneous group (tobacco, ceramics, paper board conversion, etc.).

It is very uncommon for management to keep a file of the 'light jobs' to which ailing or ageing employees can on occasion be transferred. With these firms the question could not have been so framed. It had instead to be submitted in the following form: *Please state the number of men estimated as being employed by the firm in a relatively light capacity as* . . . To widen the scope of the whole inquiry, respondents were asked to ignore any distinctions between the needs of the older manual workers of a firm and those of technically disabled or temporarily incapacitated men. There is some evidence that in several of the firms the range of light jobs already filled had about exhausted their ability to provide them, even at a stretch; but there is always a chance that if pressed an employer could spread the definition a little further.

At the time the inquiries were made, the 34 firms were employing among them an aggregate of about 111,150 male manual workers. About 61,740 were operatives, 33,770 on maintenance staffs and 15,630 on miscellaneous and ancillary jobs. The men estimated to be on relatively 'light' work would have been included under the last category. They amounted in all to 3,963.

There was no common pattern, of course, in the employment policies of the firms. The only rational plan is to assume that they are, as a group, a fair cross section of the larger manufacturing firms of the country. They are likely to foreshadow the industrial shape of things to come. In precise terms the numbers of men who were deemed to be on relatively light jobs ran as follows: Watchmen 137. Cleaners 450. Sweepers 356. Lift Attendants 67. Gardeners and Allied Workers 79. Canteen and Kitchen Hands 80. Light Boilermen 42. Messengers 110. Handymen 56. Gatekeepers 69. Parking Attendants 174. Doorkeepers 10. Car Washers and Garage Hands 47. 'Tea Boys' 25. Lavatory Attendants 352. Medical Orderlies 104. Light Labourers 718. Packers 135. Servicing Others 47. Storemen 398. Porters 31. Others Unspecified 476.

These numbers are not large. They amount to rather less than 4 per cent of the whole male manual labour force. Since there were in mid 1962 practically six million men employed in manufacture.[1] we may suppose that about 200,000 of them might have been employed, temporarily or permanently, on comparatively light work. That, however, would be to underestimate the possible proportions; many medium sized firms can probably make fuller use of such sub-standard labour.

There are two factors to be allowed for in judging what the figures imply. The first of these is the ages to which employees

[1] *Ministry of Labour Gazette*, June 1963.

continued to work; for that would show broadly with what manner of men we are dealing. Out of the 34 firms 13 had adopted a rigid rule of retiring their employees at 65 years. In a further 9 firms there was no official ruling; but to all appearance it was the accepted convention on both sides that men would withdraw at or about the same age. Managements had retained some latitude; and in half these firms extension of service depended on the outcome of a medical examination. The remaining 12 firms gave an impression that their policies were still flexible. One at least of them set the limit at 70 years; and there may have been other qualifications. But in a matter of this kind employers can often rely on accepted custom to remove ageing men who are plainly unfit for work, once they have become pensionable.

The size of a firm bore little relation to its retirement policy. But if we measure by the aggregate of manual workers in all of them, it seems that almost two thirds of the employees were bound by rule or by custom to a retiring age of 65. There is no proof, of course, that on leaving their firms such men would have failed to find another job; we were concerned only with what the manufacturing world could do about them. The firms were asked whether they made any distinct regulations for men who had been transferred to a light job. In some undertakings it is known to be the practice to retire such men at a pensionable age, though the conditions of employment are otherwise flexible. The firms approached made here no discrimination; if men remained competent on their transfer jobs, employers who had otherwise no retiring age kept them on the pay roll.

What a firm judges to be an appropriate 'transfer job' depends largely on its experience. For instance, most of the gatekeepers, doorkeepers and watchmen recorded were concentrated in a comparatively small number of the firms. We have to respect the opinion of several of the firms that security work of this type demands nowadays able-bodied men. I am further inclined to think that, as far as sweepers and cleaners are concerned, the relative lightness of the work would depend on two factors—the extent to which a firm had adopted fairly heavy machines for the purpose, and the conditions under which the work had to be carried out on the shop floor. The precise line drawn between 'heavy' and 'light' work in this regard tends to be very subjective. Elderly messengers, again, were not employed in large numbers; almost half the firms included none at all in their records. The point here is that, if internal messengers are needed in a firm, their duties are often felt to provide a useful initiation for young recruits; and in that case the work they did would certainly not be graded as 'light' in the conventional sense.

The second factor to be allowed for lies in the answer to the question, whether a firm has on its books any manual workers of the kind who are supernumerary to its strict requirements; that would usually imply that they have been retained on sympathetic grounds and would not be replaced when they left. More than half the firms could not give any estimate or did not admit that the inquiry was relevant. With the remaining 16 firms the estimates varied. They were mostly well below 1 per cent of the manual labour force. But they were sufficient to suggest that the managements concerned were probably near their economic limits in finding alternative work for those rendered unfit for normal employment. This matter of 'carrying' a few men on sympathetic grounds usually applies to the long service employees of a firm; and here the comments of one Canadian observer on the possible benefits of a fixed retiring age may be pertinent; his views would find agreement in many quarters on this side of the Atlantic. 'If the worker is to be arbitrarily released from employment at the age of 65, his chances of being kept in employment *until* he is 65 are immeasurably increased. Given no system of retirement whatsoever, and with it no sense of obligation on the part of employers to keep workers on to a certain age, the effect clearly would be . . . to reduce the number of workers in employment who had not yet attained the age of 65.'[1]

The adoption by industries of a pre-determined age of retirement is a subject that has often been discussed. Though this may be biologically and medically a very questionable policy, it cannot be denied that it has advantages for some of the men themselves. A number of them do cease to make the grade before they reach that age; and if managers and supervisors know precisely the term of years for which in each case they will have to bear with such men, they can calculate the probable costs and are the more disposed to 'carry' them in the interests of smooth industrial relations.

It has been already suggested that the quantity of unskilled labour required by industry may soon be related to the volume of amenities and services management sees fit to provide.[2] Since most of the *light* work of a plant is classified also as *unskilled*, it seems likely that the principle will hold for light jobs as well. Thus there has certainly been a recent decline of light work opportunities in packing and despatch departments, in so far as the operations involved become mechanised and so incorporated into the main flow of production. But the development of canteen services, cloak and rest rooms, gardens, car parks, etc., always tends to enlarge the volume of labour needed on ancillary work. For a while industrial services of these kinds may increase. But there is probably a limit to them; and that limit might be set by the growing recognition that the costs involved are not being matched by any equivalent rise in productivity. Whatever happens in the future, we may, I think, be sure that conventional 'light' jobs will henceforth be closely associated with those parts of a firm's activities that strictly lie outside the business of producing and despatching goods.

[1] Professor S. D. Clark, University of Toronto, *The Employability of the Older Worker: A Review of Research Findings*. Department of Labour, Ottawa, 1959.

[2] See Chapter 3.

We may now try to summarise what has been said. Even the most modern of manufacturing plants still contrive to find room for unskilled jobs that have survived under their traditional names. A proportion of these ancillary jobs could be safely committed to men who are not quite ablebodied (whatever the cause of their defects). But if we aggregate the whole manual labour force of manufacturing plants within a given area, we shall not be likely to identify more than about 4 per cent of its members as lying in that category. We may expect a large proportion of them to be already in their fifties or beyond. Though there are fashions in industry that might temporarily widen the range of these 'light' jobs, a number of technical and organisational changes are conspiring to narrow it. They are, I think, of three main kinds.

In the first place, there are few of the labouring jobs characteristic of manufacture that could not now be technically mechanised, and so (in many instances) incorporated into the sequence of factory operations. In the second place, the status of many unskilled jobs undergoes a gradual modification in the eyes of management; as often as not, they are upgraded in the process to posts that are felt to demand special qualities—i.e. a good physique, a degree of self-assurance and reliability.

Lastly, there is always a modicum of competition for these traditionally light jobs between the older employees of a firm and other suitable applicants. Not only are some jobs of the kind considered a useful first stage in the initiation of young recruits, many of whom will later graduate to operatives or supervisors; it is tacitly assumed by management that a proportion of recruits—even if only a small proportion—will remain at the labouring grade throughout their working lives. There are other sources of competition an older operative may have to face. It is the policy in many firms to recruit for security posts some of the men who are retired from the police and armed forces, the post office, etc. A large proportion of such men are both competent and medically fit; and the policy of recruiting them has some bearing on the status normally accorded to the posts they are required to fill. It must be noted that 22 out of the 34 firms approached had adopted this policy; as for those who had not, it seemed partly a matter of chance and partly due to an inclination to reserve the jobs for their own long-service employees. The majority of the men thus recruited were being employed as gatekeepers and fire security officers.

Before we decide what our evidence means, it will be as well to examine briefly the experiences of some of the non-manufacturing industries. For they can occasionally be a little more explicit about the amount of alternative work they have to offer. We have seen meanwhile that the theory that such work must somehow be available needs a good deal of qualification; certainly in the future the amount of it will not match the probable number of applicants from among the older men; their numbers will be far too large.

7 *The Assumption that Alternative Jobs must be Available*

(2) *In Non-Manufacturing Industries*

Inquiries were made in four of the non-manufacturing industries—rail transport, bus transport, coal mining and power generation. In general, the questions posed were much the same as in the manufacturing plants, i.e. *To what extent is it possible to continue to utilise the labour of men who have been rendered 'marginal' in their performance?* All that can be claimed from so limited an inquiry is that more comprehensive studies would probably arrive at quantities and proportions of a very similar order.

Rail Transport

One of the Regions of British Railways has for some years followed the practice of maintaining a central register of all 'light duty posts' at its disposal. Any men who are in need of a transfer to such posts, whether temporarily or permanently, are matched with jobs that happen at the moment to be unfilled; and a record is kept of the transactions. This gives us some chance of seeing what such an industrial undertaking can achieve in dealing with problems of the kind.

The practice would not differ much in the other Regions of B.R. They all seem to look upon the same types of work as suitable transfer jobs. A good many cases of impaired health can, of course, be handled locally; and a number of them probably do not come in the first instance to the notice of a Welfare Officer—still less to that of Headquarters. But it is felt by the Region we are here considering that a central register makes for greater flexibility and impartiality.

So widely dispersed an industry as the Railways is not like a compact manufacturing plant. Men have to be moved to alternative work near their places of residence; and where that is not feasible, the question of travelling expenses would always arise. This last problem has been complicated by the closing of intermediate stations and the consequent need to use road transport. It will thus be appreciated that most of the light duty posts mentioned are peculiar to rail conditions.

At the time of the inquiry the Region was employing about 45,000 men on its line traffic operations; in addition there were some 9,600 on permanent way maintenance, 7,500 in the workshops and 5,400 on miscellaneous loading and maintenance operations. Only in a very slight degree could transfers be effected from one department to another.

We will now aggregate all the 'light duty posts' recorded in the central register. They amounted to 1,659. That represents about 2·7 per cent of the whole manual labour force of the Region (omitting a few small and specialised departments). It will be noted that the proportion is not far short of that estimated in the last chapter for a sample of manufacturing firms.

On the railways the course of transfer to light duties was necessarily restricted. Thus men on the permanent way (i.e. lengthmen, relayers, etc.) might in theory be offered the alternative jobs of point oilers, flagmen or look-out men; failing that, they might be accommodated as mess-room attendants or sweepers. The number of posts of this nature was 204. Porters, on the other hand, would normally be transferred to the work of messengers or letter sorters, if there were any such vacancies; otherwise they too would have to undertake cleaning or mess-room duties. Higher grade porters, however, would probably have to be considered for the work of store-keepers or luggage room attendants; or they might indeed become ticket collectors. For though the post of ticket collector is a promotion job, it is often relatively 'light' in its demands on a man. As a matter of fact, 240 such posts were reckoned as suitable transfer placings—most of them of course on the smaller stations.

Some signalmen still had the chance of settling down as resident crossing keepers. Indeed, this must at the time have been the largest of all the transfer categories, since there were 346 listed in the register. For the rest, there were in the depots a few specific tasks such as those of lamp men and telephone attendants; and on goods porterage there were the duties of time keeper and weighbridgemen. But if all the accessible jobs of the kinds mentioned were already filled, a man might have to accept the job of a gatekeeper, sweeper, lavatory attendant, etc.

So much for the common run of 'light duty posts' on the railways. A transfer to any one of them usually means a loss of pay; but an agreement with the Union has established the man's new wage level at somewhere about half way between his original pay and that normally appropriate to his transfer status. In the nature of things, however, it is never easy to match an applicant with a job that would suit him in every respect. At the time of the inquiry, for example, only about 85 per cent of recorded applicants had been accommodated; some of them were still convalescent and about 5 per cent were on the waiting list. In addition, about 7 per cent were understood to be on 'considerate work', a term implying that adjustments had been locally made pending a formal transfer.

The railways share with several other industries the medical practice of rehabilitating sick or injured men in their place of work; and this undoubtedly means that a proportion of the light posts would go to men who are only temporarily incapacitated. It was estimated that these men might represent up to 15 per cent of the average number of transfers recorded. The remainder were likely to be permanent cases; and at least two out of three of these must have been aged 55 and over. On the railways a retirement age had not at the time been rigidly applied (except in the case of engine drivers), though retirement at 65 often takes place by accepted ruling or custom. What we have to observe is that the supply of light work shows no signs of increasing. In the process of rationalisation it might very well diminish.

Bus Transport

One of the large Bus Companies has adopted a similar register of light posts. The expedient is presumably more useful in a Service in which about 83 per cent of the manual grades are employed as drivers or conductors. The number of men in the Company's employment on its Central Buses was about 29,000. 14,000 of these were drivers; and the male conductors amounted to about 9,500. About 5,100 men worked in the garages and on other operations.

The register of the light work at the Company's disposal listed 937 jobs. That is about 3·2 per cent of the pay roll—again a proportion close to the proportions already discussed. What with the widely dispersed homes of the men concerned and the limited range of light jobs, the Company obviously has the same problem as have the railways in attempting to match the applicants with the vacant posts.

A good many of the duties classified as 'light' were more or less static; but some of them were mobile. Thus about 200 of the men were 'pointsmen', messengers, etc.; and a further 100 moved here and there recording the variable numbers of passengers and other relevant information. About 140 acted as departmental messengers. The remainder of the transferred men (apart from about 50 employed as lift attendants, hall porters and the rest room cleaners), would have been in the garages.

It is probable that the proportion of men who come to need such preferential treatment is somewhat higher on the buses than in most forms of manufacture. After all, a driver cannot moderate his efforts; and a conductor has to be capable of carrying out his full duties.

An earlier report on the Service[1] examining the records of men who had passed the age of 60 and then continued with the

[1] *Bus Workers in their Later Lives*. The Nuffield Foundation 1957.

Company for a further five years or more, concluded that about 15 per cent in their early sixties had been thus transferred. Even before the age of 60 a number of men have to be taken off driving, though it is likely that a fair proportion of these subsequently leave the Service to seek work elsewhere. Most of the available 'light' jobs are, in fact, reserved for long service employees. It was rare, however, for all applicants to be suited; thus in the year 1952–3 about 13 per cent of them were not and apparently could not be re-absorbed into the Service.

Under these conditions it is not surprising that a Company, that was prepared to retain men in normal work beyond 65 (subject to a periodic medical examination), found it necessary to impose a retiring age on those who had been transferred to some alternative work. There were fresh applicants for the jobs every year; and it seemed imperative to clear the field. Besides, a certain proportion of the 'light jobs' of an undertaking would often be judged supernumerary by any strict costs accountancy. It appeared, indeed, at the time of the inquiry that, if one in nine of the transferred men decided to leave the Company, he would not need to be replaced. He was being retained, in other words, mainly on sympathetic grounds. We must recognise, in short, that it may become as inconvenient for a firm to have the way blocked to its supply of 'light jobs' as it is to have the way blocked on its conventional promotion ladder; in both cases a retirement ruling seems the only course to adopt.

Coal Mining

I know of no Division of the Coal Board that maintains a comparable register of light duties. It has been the custom for each colliery to re-deploy partially incapacitated men in its own way. Normally the proportion of transfers that have to be effected is not very large. But there is always some drift of men from the coal face by reason of age; and this drift crosses the movement of young recruits towards the coal face. The age at which a young miner graduates to the status of a coal getter varies from one part of the country to another; but the age of 19 or so would be usual in the technically advanced Divisions.

It is possible, however, to make an estimate of the amount of light work that would be available in a colliery. For this purpose we have to take a colliery that is already at a fairly advanced stage of mechanisation; and since the process of mechanisation is still going on, the situation is bound to change.

In the colliery studied there were a few faces where coal was still being loaded by hand on to the conveyor belts, and where the roof was supported by the conventional method of 'packing' fallen rock. More than 25 per cent of all men at the coal faces were, in fact, 'packers'. But the replacement of all this by cutter-loader machines and movable props effectively reduces the numbers of men required. At the time there were about 70 men per shift on the machines at the coal face; and it was suggested that possibly 4 or these could have been less than thoroughly able-bodied. A further 70 men were employed on the operations involved in checking the steel supports, repairing belts etc.; about 6 of these might have been less than able-bodied. But the definition is only one of degree; how far a man could really be 'sub-standard' in any one case would be a matter of opinion on the part of management.

For the rest of the coal face work, including the preparation of each end of a long wall and the removal of the lip of overhead rock left as the 'gates' advanced, all colliers had to be well up to standard. Thus the face workings of a mine could at most draw 2 per cent of the labour needed from among 'less fit' operatives; and any physical impairment such men experienced would have to be of minor importance. Much of it would only be a matter of temporary labour adjustments.

Elsewhere below ground, however, one finds a number of jobs that would be traditionally described as light. About 360 men (apart from craftsmen and officials) were employed in this part of the colliery. A variable proportion of them—perhaps 17–20 per cent—were developing new roadways, raising roof levels, lowering floors, etc. Most of the work demanded consistent effort. The only possible exception to this was the task of 'back-ripping', i.e. raising roofs immediately behind the face, where speed is less important; the job seemed often to be left to a few of the older colliers. More than half the 360 men were on transport. Though experience suggests that the majority of them were young miners in their stage of initiation, there were a few jobs (especially on the trams) that could be committed to slightly disabled men. It was commoner, however, for men of this kind to be placed on a diversity of maintenance and safety operations, e.g. duties on the supply and haulage system, duties at transfer points on the conveyor belts, stone-dusting for the suppression of coal dust.

In all, it might be reckoned that back of the coal face underground the labour force could be diluted with 10 per cent or so of men who, through age or some other cause, showed a decline in their working capacity. But in many instances 'working capacity' would here mean the level of strenuous effort demanded at the coal face; men would still have to be reasonably fit and mobile.

About a quarter of the surface workers of the colliery were craftsmen, or else employed on duties that called for a high degree of responsibility or muscular strength. In addition one has to allow for a number of winders, drivers, banksmen, etc. But at the time about a third of the surface men were employed on the coal washeries or the screens, and in general labouring. It was among these latter jobs that a proportion of ageing or ailing men would normally be found. The least suitable work was probably that of general labouring; while a few older men were to be met on it, they were often able-bodied individuals who had gravitated there from other industries. Meanwhile, it must be noted that the mechanical washing of coal, though it has certainly lightened the effort, limits the number of men required on the process. A counterbalancing factor is the larger volume of coal that can now be raised to the surface; and this might for a period help to maintain the numbers employed on washing and screening.

It is thus difficult to estimate how many of the 'less fit' men could be infused into the surface labour of a colliery. But it seems probable that about 15 per cent of those on 'partly skilled' operations could be included under that category.

There is, of course, nothing constant about coal mining. I can only say that in a colliery, that was at least 80 per cent mechanised, it seemed possible to fill 7 or 8 per cent of all the definable jobs with men who would not have been capable of working at the coal face; and their diminished capacity might be due to age or injury or some other cause. But it is easiest to trace out the probable effects of age, whether or not it is complicated by injury or ill health. Beyond the age of 50 a drift from the coal face usually becomes noticeable. To observe what was apparently happening, I took the numbers of men working in seven collieries as they were classified in age groups and by the areas of the collieries in which they were employed. Their numbers were recorded in five-year age groups; and I took them for the years 1956 and 1961. By the year 1956 each of the seven collieries was already moving into a stage of fairly advanced mechanisation; so that working conditions in the two years studied would not have been dissimilar.

The simple method adopted was this. Five years elapsed between the two sets of recorded numbers; and it follows that by the close of that period every man would have been five years older. To what extent had they been transferred in the interval of time from one area of the colliery to another, e.g. from work at the coal face to work on the surface?

We know, of course, that the men recorded in 1961 would not necessarily have been the same men as those who had been recorded in 1956. A few, even in their fifties, might move from one colliery to another; and where men vanish, they might have died or become invalids or departed for a variety of reasons. Thus the percentages of gains and losses in the following Table only provide a broad picture of the course of events. In balance men were being replaced at the coal face, as they grew old, by an inflow of young recruits; and in balance again, labour elsewhere in the colliery was being supplemented by men of roughly the same advanced ages. Precise numbers are not relevant. It will be sufficient to show the proportionate increases or decreases in the three main areas of mine working.

Table X

APPROXIMATE PERCENTAGE INCREASES OR DECREASES IN NUMBERS (OVER A FIVE YEAR PERIOD) OF COHORTS OF MEN EMPLOYED IN MINING AT THE AGES INDICATED

Ages in 1956		46–50	51–55	56–60
Ages in 1961		*51–55*	*56–60*	*60–64*
Per cent changes of numbers by 1961	Coal Face	−32	−48	−56
	Elsewhere below ground	+19	+15	−16
	Surface	+ 9	+ 7	−23

The losses of men from the last age group, whether below ground or on the surface, were due to the fact that mortality and premature invalidity would then have been making a consistent inroad into their numbers. Some of the men, aware that they would be retired at 65, would have been disposed to seek work elsewhere.

It has been suggested by the Coal Board that the gradual mechanisation of coal-getting is having the effect of slowing down the rate at which older colliers leave the coal face. The only serious consequence this might have is that it would retard the rate at which young men can be promoted to the higher paid work; and this in turn could lead to an increase in the rate of labour turnover. But I have little evidence that mechanisation is so far producing much of a change in this respect. As a matter of fact, similar records taken from six 'low mechanised' collieries in the same Division and over the same term of years show that movements from the coal face had been negligible among the men who were passing from their late forties into their early fifties. The wastage at still later ages was well below the rates of wastage in the mechanised mines.

We have seen that the collieries have still a fair amount of latitude by way of finding appropriate work for those in need, and that in all probability without carrying much supernumerary labour. It was noted in an earlier chapter that in 1961 a compulsory retiring age was imposed by the industry. This not only helped to soften the impact of redundancies; it would have relieved in some measure the task of providing suitably 'light' work. As matters stand at present, if decisions are ever taken to remove men from the coal face at predetermined ages, or to associate their re-deployment otherwise with age, such a policy will have little to do with their continued average fitness; it will have much more bearing on the need to ensure a steady flow of young labour to the coal face. It must be remembered, however, that if mining seems to have a larger supply of 'light jobs' than many other industries, this is in reality because we are judging the fitness of the men by the exacting standards of coal face work; the relatively light jobs available are not all that light, as compared with most of the light work that would be offered an older factory employee.

Power Generation

Annual reports of the National Joint Advisory Councils of the Electrical Industry have referred incidentally to a concern felt for the rehabilitation of men affected by illness, accident or approaching old age. In one place the suggestion was advanced that the industry should have sufficient man-power flexibility to enable management to provide selective employment for disabled men, in excess of the establishment laid down. This has the appearance of being a minor item in the protracted efforts of the Unions to reconcile man-power requirements in a changing technology with working conditions that would satisfy the needs of the men employed. In point of fact, that is the underlying problem now likely to confront a number of industries; sooner or later a man-power formula has to be reached based in reality on the size of a pay roll *in excess of the labour theoretically required* for the effective running of a plant. The *excess* man-power would represent, of course, the level at which employees are prepared to bargain to carry out a fair and full week's work.

There is no indication that much has been so far done to meet this special demand in the electrical industry. The generating side of the industry has few physical risks; and it has still a relatively young age structure. There is, moreover, a technical retiring age of 65; and though that is not always rigidly applied, it does at least set a term to the problem. It seems to me that there are two operative areas that would demand some attention. The first is thoroughly concrete—the fact that power generation is defined as including the maintenance of high transmission lines on the grid. The second is still largely hypothetical—the precise degree of strain that might be imposed on the *mental* resources of a man who has continually to operate with a complex automatic installation.

A limited inquiry was made about the duties of linesmen on the transmission system. Their numbers are relatively small—approximately 1 per cent of manual grades employed in power generation. No ruling had at the time been found necessary in regard to their age. The ages at which the men left climbing duties seemed too widely distributed for it to be associated directly with senescence. Figures for the last few years suggested that on average about 1 per cent of them were being annually transferred to other work; but reasons varied considerably. Thus of a series of eleven transfers five, where the ages ranged from 35 to 48, had been effected at the men's own requests; three other linesmen aged 33 to 40, had been moved on medical grounds.

A list of the jobs with which such men were accommodated showed no clear pattern. Most of them were apparently placed on auxiliary work in the transmission section, e.g. as linesmen's or fitter's mates, storemen, route wardens and safety men. Even if the numbers provided with posts of this kind may on occasion become uneconomically high, they are unlikely to add much to the pay roll. The two factors now giving some concern to the Authority are the changing age structure of men employed on the transmission lines, and the relative height of the new towers. The combination of these factors may initiate a change of policy.

In the power stations themselves the operative staff is comparatively small. A station would employ a labouring pool on various unskilled or semi-skilled jobs, amounting perhaps to about 3 per cent of its manual workers; and such a pool could in theory absorb a few older men. There is, moreover, nothing to prevent a man from transferring from the generating to the distributing side of his industry; but though such transfers do take place, there seems no evidence as to their frequency.

The relative functions carried out by members of the operative staff are most commonly settled through a system of promotions. A man might enter the service as a shift labourer, and then move up from grade to grade with the hope of ultimately becoming a unit controller. In practice the promotion ladder need not preclude an experienced operative from taking over temporarily the duties of the grade next above his own; in that way the continuous running of the station can be ensured in case of a fortuitous sickness or accident. But such emergencies would be of rare occurrence.

Power generation is one of the industries in which the question of an older man's continued effectiveness is likely to present itself in a novel form; and for that reason a few preliminary remarks are worth making. More will be said later about this very pertinent problem. Let me get to the essential point. Traditionally the manual worker has had to meet the physical test involved in negotiating heavy loads, keeping pace with a working gang or maintaining a steady rate of output. Any failure to do so was usually noticed; and it could often be precisely measured. But when men are operating with semi-automatic or automatic installations, the signs of a change in their level of performance are far less readily observed. The natural supposition is that, unless a man's muscular strength or perhaps his sense organs are demonstrably affected, he is not growing old in any strict meaning of the term.

Yet there is evidence that changes of a deep-seated kind are simultaneously taking place in a man's mental mechanism, and presumably also in his central nervous system. The symptoms are rarely obtrusive; and they may vary a little from man to man. They are not likely to occur to a man in the prime of life. The vague consciousness that one is losing mental assurance is a commonplace accompaniment of age.

At a venture I suggest that in a power station the testing time could come, for instance, where a man has to deal with variable sequences of adjustment or make a series of rapid decisions that do not follow a routine pattern. Under such conditions a unit controller would have to hold in a short-span memory his awareness that all the successive steps required have been carried out. That these crises are infrequent does not alter the fact that they may occur. The structure of inter-related duties in a power station means that responsibility resides less with a single individual than with the whole team. Though an assistant controller or one of the auxiliary attendants in the plant is usually engaged on routine duties or acting under orders, he is almost as sensible as the unit controller himself of the warning signals and the variable adjustments that have to be made. Thus we can say that an accepted retiring age of 65 makes it very improbable that *mental* senescence alone will ever be much of a problem. But any extension of employment beyond that age might run into difficulties.

However, in the generating industry the idea of 'alternative work' does not seem entirely applicable. In this and in comparable industries we may find that the Unions will agree to the principle that an older operative shall occasionally be 'demoted' without loss of pay; but that principle does not appear to be at present recognised outside the limits of the Civil Service. We have to see the newer industrial forms as still working out, through a process of negotiations, the most appropriate relationship between one operative grade and the next, and probably that between operative and maintenance staffs; for the status of maintenance workers in the new industries is also in the melting pot.

What tentative conclusions can be drawn from the last two chapters? I began them by noting references in official reports to various industrial jobs that are deemed to be in the nature of light or alternative work. It was assumed that, when supervisors have to discard men from an organised department, a good many of them could be transferred to such jobs. Now, it is true that this practice had been followed in industry for generations. Several of the light jobs recorded were known in mediaeval times. It was never indeed claimed that all in need of attention could be thus accommodated; but occupational statistics certainly show that most jobs of the kind used formerly to absorb considerable numbers of men within the older age range.

The basic question is whether such jobs are likely to become less available than they were in the past; for if they do, it will be far more difficult to deal with the human wastage of industry. Our first suspicion that this may be the case arises from the evidence that some industrial undertakings admit to employing on these jobs a small margin of supernumerary labour; in other words, there are older men whose jobs would not be filled, once they left a firm. They usually represent too small a percentage of the pay roll to trouble management. But this is a time of industrial rationalisation; and that may have two results. For one thing, an effort to avoid redundancies might lead to the transfer of a few of the less adapable middle-aged men to unskilled work; and if there is some guarantee of a maintenance of basic wage levels, any supernumerary labour among the unskilled grades would certainly attract notice. For another, the elementary urge to rationalise an undertaking is bound (in a competitive world) to reach down into the 'light work' category sooner or later.

But the most important long-term effect of rationalisation is the way in which much of the work, that could formerly have been reserved for ageing or ailing employees, is being gradually assimilated to the mechanised processes of production. This could apply to a fair amount of the servicing, packing, despatch and stores operations of a plant. Once a job has been partly mechanised, it is usually capable of further technical refinements; in any case it ceases to be work appropriate for a man who is by any definition 'slowing down'.

There are possibly two main kinds of industrial work that cannot be so easily mechanised. One of these might be represented by a despatch department wherein a firm wholesales a large variety of products or components, and needs for that reason to fulfil a long series of mixed orders; in such a case it is impracticable to mechanise the collections of products and the subsequent packing operations. Older men are, in fact, often employed on the work. The other exception is what are commonly termed the 'nuisance jobs' of a plant, i.e. the salvaging and sorting of scrap metal, the scouring and reconditioning of containers, etc.; all this kind of work can be economically left to men who are going to move circumspectly and at their own pace. It might indeed be quite uneconomic to replace unskilled human labour for the purpose by any mechanical device.

With regard to the various amenities that many firms have thought fit to adopt (canteens, club rooms, sports grounds, etc.) it is clear that, if these continue to expand, they could in theory provide work for a fair number of older men. But I am doubtful to what extent many of them will survive in their present form. Medical departments will develop further; and so in many instance will personnel departments. Most of the other industrial amenities and benefits are failing, as it seems to me, to typify the basic satisfactions the average employee wants to get out of his job. Those satisfactions must be embodied, if they are embodied anywhere, in the job itself. They must mean that an employee has reached at least a temporary agreement with management as to what constitutes a fair week's work;

and in the last resort *a fair week's work*, let us begin to admit, is what he and his working team decide collectively to be 'fair'. In a way most industrial emenities are acceptable to an employee, but they are not of the essence of his relation to the job itself. Many similar or better amenities could in practice grow up outside a plant, as part of the ordinary commercial or municipal life of a community; and for all I know the average employee would prefer it that way.

I have suggested that the amount of 'light work' available in a plant will depend henceforth directly on the extent to which management interests itself in the provision of such amenities. But management is far more concerned nowadays with *job satisfactions* on the shop floor, on the building site or at the coal face. This concern stems from a growing awareness that, when men are organised for production, they always tend to organise among them their own codes of industrial morality in regard to work schedules and group solidarity; it is with these employee codes of right conduct and fair bargaining that management has ultimately to come to terms. In consequence, more attention is being paid than ever before to such matters as factory hygiene, work hazards, working rhythms, the domestic worries of employees and the rehabilitation of convalescents in their normal place of work. As a further result, the 'sub-standard' employee who has become a *permanent* casualty no longer fits so easily into the pattern of industrial welfare; his very existence is becoming something of a dilemma to managers and supervisors. He may even be competing for the available 'light jobs' that management prefers to reserve for other claimants, e.g. for men on the pay roll who are recovering after an injury or a bout of illness. Managers and trade unionists acknowledge that they have obligations towards a long-service employee; the trouble is that they can see no simple means of implementing them.

This competitive element in the field of 'light work' is sufficiently important in modern industry to make it worth our while to examine the extent to which it may emerge in the life of a factory. It is closely associated, of course, with the duties of an Industrial Medical Officer, since he has to advise as to suitable forms of industrial rehabilitation.

ANNOTATION TO CHAPTERS 6 AND 7

Relevance of the Increasing use of 'Light Work' in Industrial Rehabilitation

In his advisory function the industrial doctor now plays an important role; and it is not improbable that industrial medicine will in time become co-extensive with industry and commerce. Among his duties would be that of advising what form of work is suitable for the rehabilitation of a convalescent employee after injury, sickness or surgical treatment. In fact it is only in the presence of a medical officer that it would become safe to attempt such rehabilitation *in the Works*. While many men want to get back to a job as soon as they can earn good money, medical supervision is necessary; and on that point some at least of the Trade Unions are properly sensitive. As far as numbers are concerned the problem is not a very large one. It has nevertheless a direct bearing on the availability of 'light work' in modern industry.

Preliminary inquiries were accordingly made from a number of Industrial Medical Officers through the medium of the Office of Health Economics. The outcome would show, it was hoped, whether a more detailed study of industrial rehabilitation might subsequently be useful. But the findings are analysed in the present context because of the bearing they plainly have upon the problem of alternative work.

Medical Officers were approached through their own Association. Only 207 returned the completed forms of inquiry, of whom 49 indicated that in their industries the questions were not appropriate. However, several members of the Association are in the Factory Inspectorate; and since (at our suggestion) a number of senior Medical Officers had nominated the doctor of a single plant among many to reply, it was clear that an uncertain proportion of members were thus automatically excluded from our sample. The 158 Medical Officers who completed the form recorded the numbers of employees for whom they were responsible. In that several gave the figures in round numbers, they will here be shown approximately. There were 1,501,000 males and 236,700 females. The character of the industries made it inevitable that the sample of male employees would be disproportionately high.

One respondent gave no information about the nature of his industry. The distribution of the remaining 157 was as follows: Engineering 52, Chemical and Pharmaceutical industries 32, Electricity, Gas and Water 18, Metal Manufacture 15, Transport (all forms) 14, Food Processing 9, Mining 5, Miscellaneous (mainly Commercial) 8. It had been recognised that some of the questions would not be applicable to all fields of employment; and to a varied extent a few respondents refrained from an expression of views. The information is sufficiently comprehensive, however, to warrant us in attempting some provisional inferences from it.

The inquiry was confined to *rehabilitation within the Works*, i.e. to the recommending of such alternative jobs as would be appropriate to the condition of a convalescent employee. Thus it was explicitly asked that no regard should be paid to special 'rehabilitation workshops'—or, by implication, to therapeutic exercises in a clinic or in a man's own hope. Moreover, men whose working capacity had been *permanently* impaired were not to be included; it was to be assumed that the convalescents would subsequently resume their normal duties or the equivalent of them. To the question whether their firms found light or modified work for such men, 88 of the 158 I.M.O.s replied that this was very often the case and 58 that the practice was a fairly common one. It was rare in 9 cases and non-existent in 3.

On two aspects of the matter medical opinions were sought. The I.M.O.s were asked whether they considered the practice of rehabilitating men at work is medically advisable. Since the majority of them had adopted the practice, it was obvious that the replies would usually be in the affirmative. All but 4 of the 158 held it to be advisable. Those who did not favour it were admittedly thinking of conditions in their own industries. The other query related to the possible advantages of such treatment to the employee himself. We had been doubtful whether the benefit, provided the work undertaken was medically fitted to a man's condition, would not often be as much psychological as merely physical; any physical benefit that accrued might just as well be gained by a course of occupational therapy. Most of the respondents, however, assumed that the advantage was a combination of both elements; and that, of course, is an undeniably sound position to adopt. Only eight thought the effects were mainly psychological.

As for a man's own feeling that, once he is so far recovered, a resumption of work rhythms would be advisable or even a source of satisfaction—here, one might surmise, employees vary considerably. It is thought, in some industries (probably with reason) that such factors as the level of his sickness pay and the assured security of his job would usually influence a man's decisions. I have no immediate evidence that this is the rule, though Managers in a Nationalised Industry have tended to assume it. In answer to a question whether in the experience of the I.M.O.s convalescents preferred rehabilitation in their place of work to being off work until fit, almost 45 per cent replied that preferences varied too widely to allow of an opinion. But 58 of the 158 I.M.O.s thought that men preferred a return to work of some kind; and 30 said men would prefer to remain off work until fit for their normal duties. Thus in about a third of the plants there seemed a bias among employees towards rehabilitation on a job.

The possible significance to the men of their sickness pay suggested a query about the policy of industrial firms. It was asked—'is it the policy to make up the sickness benefit of an absent convalescent to approximately his basic wage for a certain period of time?' There was no common policy, but a fairly general disposition to adopt this principle. While 26 of the 158 firms had no such scheme, 74 (i.e. almost 50 per cent) made up a man's full basic pay for a variable number of weeks. In 38 further cases the scheme applied to staff employees only; and 5 had a contributory scheme that would guarantee some addition to the statutory payment. There were 15 firms that appeared to have some variant of the scheme; and these cannot be precisely classified. About half of them, for instance, indicated that to qualify, a man would have to complete several years of service; and others allotted grants of money, that did not however make up the basic wage. One or two firms made up the wage of selected grades, though they did not state the basis of selection. We are not concerned here to trace the origin and meaning of all these arrangements; though that might be worth a study. The period of weeks or months, during which payments were guaranteed, followed no obvious pattern. Periods of 13 or 26 weeks were not uncommon. In some instances the number of weeks was related to a man's length of service; and in others his case would be reviewed after a stated period had elapsed. A distinction was frequently made between staff and manual employees, even where manual workers had been included in the scheme. What association may exist between policies of this kind and a convalescent's wish to get back to his place of work, has to be left undecided. It must be remembered that the earnings level to which a convalescent might attain, even on a modified job, could exceed his basic pay; and there is always the less tangible satisfaction some men feel in escaping from the tedium of a prolonged convalescence.[1]

It was pertinent to know something about the procedure of firms in regard to rehabilitation arrangements. In answer to the question whether a firm had any plan for encouraging a man to

[1] According to information in possession of the T.U.C. in the years 1961–62 about 56 per cent of insured men were covered by industrial sickness schemes. Payment in about a third of the cases was guaranteed for 13 weeks or less; in rather more than a quarter the period was between 13 and 26 weeks. Almost a quarter of the schemes implied that payment was to be at the discretion of the firms.

come back for rehabilitation, 63 of the I.M.O.s said that to some extent they informed individual convalescents. About 84 simply relied on a common knowledge among employees; and it is plain in any case that an awareness of the possibility would soon become general. An additional subject of interest was the relation between an I.M.O. and the medical practitioners of the neighbourhood. A G.P. is often unfamiliar with the precise characteristics of a man's work; and he would probably be easier in his mind if he knew that the 'light work' undertaken was to be under medical supervision. The I.M.O.s were uncertain in 23 cases whether their firms had any procedure for informing practitioners of the service; and 91 took it for granted that they got to know informally. But 39 (about 25 per cent) said that local practitioners were generally informed; and it must be supposed that in several instances this implied some systematic communication. For the remaining I.M.O.s the question was irrelevant since they had no plans for rehabilitation.

An attempt was then made to distinguish what trends there were, if any, in this department of industrial policy—what rehabilitation amounted to in quantitative terms. Had there been any increase over the last ten years in the custom of rehabilitating men *within the Works*? For 25 of the 158 I.M.O.s the question had no meaning or could not be answered with any degree of certainty. No marked increase was reported by 55 of them; but a considerable proportion of these added that the practice had already been well established ten years ago. In the opinion of 75 I.M.O.s rehabilitation had been growing over the period. Thus we may say that two out of three of the firms either had the practice well established by the early 'fifties and felt little need to extend it, or else had developed it significantly in more recent years. This of course has some bearing on the attention firms can pay to such matters as the provision of 'light' or modified work, and in particular *on the types of employees for whom work of the kind would be reserved.*

The quantitative problem is plainly a difficult one to approach, unless through an industrial survey continued over two or three years. We therefore only asked I.M.O.s to record any estimate that they themselves or a Personnel Department could give of the total number of convalescent employees their firms had employed on rehabilitation jobs in the course of 1963. The number of those who ventured an estimate was 99. Since we assumed on general evidence that the large majority of returned convalescents would have been males, we decided to take the figures as a ratio of the total number of male employees in these 99 firms. That total amounted to 387,000. The number of recorded rehabilitations was 8,989. This gives an annual ratio of about 2·3 to every 100 male employees. The proportion is small, especially as we have no indication at present of the *average* length of time of a man's rehabilitation. That would probably vary from a few days to a term of months. Moreover there was bound to have been an element of guesswork in some of the estimates. At most, we might conjecture that, in industries that have specifically adopted the rehabilitation principle, a proportion of 0·5 to 1·0 per cent of male employees are being at any moment provided with temporary 'light' work pending their return to normal duties.

But viewed in relation to the *overall* amount of modified work industries can make available, the proportion may not be as insignificant as it appears. We arrived earlier at estimates of, say, 3 per cent or 4 per cent of the pay roll as representing about the limit of such work that management could offer on average. If the practice of rehabilitating younger and otherwise able-bodied men seems of increasing importance to both sides of industry, the 'light duties' available in a firm would be more and more commonly reserved for that purpose by mutual agreement. There are, of course, provisos to be observed. For instance, the kind of work offered to an older long-service employee might not be of precisely the same quality as that offered to a young convalescent. But we have to face the fact that some competition is involved, and that the range of jobs open to older men may be slowly contracting.

What has been said on the subject is in reality only part of the general trend in modern industry that I have frequently noted, i.e. the marked extent to which both Managements and Trade Unions are concerned nowadays for the welfare and satisfaction of those men and women who are actually at work. Even if they had the will to interest themselves in extraneous social problems, I doubt whether they would find the time or the corporate energy. Though they are both well aware, for instance, of the need to establish adequate pension levels, they certainly give the matter far less thought at present than they do to the working out of a uniform sickness payment scheme. The trend coincides, one may say, with that other trend in industrial thinking which argues that, because some at least of the older men have to be placed on preferential work before they are 65, the most economic plan is to let it be understood that men will be kept on to a pre-determined age but not beyond that age.

8 *The Effect of Shifting the Physical Work-Load on to Machinery*

The assumption is still prevalent in Trade Union and other circles, that the rate at which a man 'ages' industrially must vary *on average* with the strain of the work-load on his muscles, joints and sense organs. The more the work-load is shifted on to a mechanised system, the longer *on average* he should be able to survive at a job. Down to a definable stage in our industrial history this was probably true; an older employee could have had the appearance of being organically 'worn out' by a lifetime of heavy labour. We have now to consider whether it remains true of contemporary industry.

The mental (as contrasted with the physical) aspects of industrial ageing were studied in the Cambridge Psychological Laboratory and elsewhere, mainly between 1946 and 1956. The findings of research have had an industrial as well as a theoretical significance, because it is evident that they are influencing managerial policy.

Many industrial processes will become in time either semi-automatic or automatic. When the machines of a department are semi-automatic, operatives are to that extent no longer exerting themselves physically in the manipulation of materials or components; they are in varying degrees servicing, driving, controlling or monitoring machines. But an operative would still have his responsibilities. For instance, in driving a stationary machine he might be required to modify its speed as, e.g. the materials being processed are reeled on or off the drums. The servicing of a machine, again, might involve feeding or taking off components in a continuous rhythm; and this might be associated with the transitory inspection of each unit handled. Being in charge of a large installation may call for the adjustment of remote controls in response to machine signals.

Moreover, until a machine is so automatic that it can forestall a mechanical or electronic breakdown by switching the production process into a spare channel, the whole working team of a department must be prepared for prompt action in dealing with an emergency.

What we have to distinguish are the human deficiencies that might incline management to take an operative *off* work of these kinds. Such human deficiencies might in theory be observed, or they may be merely suspected; and in any case they are most commonly associated with a man's age. I will comment shortly on a few factory jobs and on the ways in which they are related to the standards by which a man's continued employability would be judged.

Take first the mental qualities needed in 'feeding' a machine. Though the manual work could in many cases be now replaced by mechanical feeding, it can still be examined as a typical job. The rhythmical pace of a man's movements must depend on the rate at which the machine shapes or assembles the parts it is designed to produce; and he may be able to vary his pace by the expedient of building up small 'banks' of units. But his work is necessarily repetitive; and we have to consider whether any known psychological changes would ultimately tend to unfit him for such minimal responsibility.

The job means that each cycle of movements he makes, though it is practically identical with the cycle that preceded it, has to be gone through as one complete sequence of co-ordinations. The operative has, as it were, to re-establish the full pitch of attention to what he is doing between one cycle and the next. This may seem easy enough; but in fact his will to maintain an unremitting attention is always working against a possible background of external distractions, and of the internal distractions that are commonly thought of as day-dreaming or as intrusive thoughts with a strong emotional colouring. Do these distractions gradually intensify as age advances? As for the effect we usually expect age to have on a worker's staying power, such things as increased fatigueability or boredom vary widely in their onset. In many instances they do not seem to account for a man's apparent failings of attention. Indeed, no increase in boredom may be evident at all. The only question of importance to us is whether purely *mental* or *cerebral* changes are likely to affect a man's powers of attention —changes that are perhaps normally characteristic of later life. For if so, we can no longer explain industrial senescence simply in terms of a growing tendency to muscular or sensory fatigue.

Now, a characteristic common to all men of advancing years is the vast reserve of available memory images they have been accumulating. Such images are available in the sense only that they have not been lost altogether. But what difference does that make to a man as a machine operative? The answer is that his mind must not be conceived as a system of files or storage boxes wherein all memory images remain static until they are needed. They have something of a dynamic quality; and in consequence memories seem to manifest themselves spontaneously as transient streams of recollection, flights of surmise, daydreams and fragmented past emotions. All these are normal enough in a long-lived man. Thus the problem is whether a gradual intensification of such normal experiences will lower a man's powers of concentration at repetitive work.

When a man feels that his attentiveness is wandering, he may interpret it as a symptom of increasing strain or fatigue-ability; or he may ascribe it to the atmospheric conditions under which he is working. He may then, of course, make greater efforts to fix his attention on the work in hand. But he has always to be *noticing* what he is doing in order to satisfy himself that he has completed each successive cycle of operations; and the fact is that, where the operations carried out become too elementary or monotonous, the distinction between noticing and failing to notice what he is doing is apt to be blurred by any interruptions of his attention. I suggest that the main source of such interruptions is the increased liveliness of his mind as age advances, i.e. the increased tendency of memory and other images to overflow uninvited into his consciousness. It is presumably a form of psychological adaptation such as we must expect to pay for the privilege of a long life. The only thing that can be said in its disfavour is that it is a form of adaptation not well suited to the demands of modern industry. It renders most men past 60 less and less reliable on repetitive work, where little physical effort is needed; for physical effort involving the whole muscular system at least helps to stabilize a man's attention to what he is doing.

Much the same might apply to an operator at the controls of a semi-automatic installation. The number of possible combinations, for which he has to be prepared, are not unlimited; and experience would, of course, have made him a master of them. The human capacity for memorising the relevant complexities of a machine system is obviously very large; and it is on this that a machine designer relies when he has to consider whether the human factor will be equal to managing or piloting a new machine.

What happens when an experienced man settles down each day to such work is that his mind is immediately screwed up, so to speak, to an adequate level of tonicity; all the possible combinations he may have to deal with are poised in mental suspension. Provided his health and his organs remain unimpaired, it would not be easy to say when to expect a deterioration in his proved ability to carry out his duties. But there are grounds for thinking that with age a man's range of attentiveness inclines to narrow somewhat. His attention 'flickers', as it were, rather more often than it formerly did, in the sense that after a momentary lapse he will come back to the work in hand and deal with it *almost* as expeditiously as was once his habit. But there may be slight delays in his reaction to signals.

It is not that such a man grows unaware that emergencies are possible, but rather that he is becoming a little less prepared mentally to meet them if they do occur. He may have begun to assume that his reactions will always be automatic and effective

—whereas, if the testing moment did come, that might not be the case. There are other symptoms of senescence, that may only be observed in their inception by the man himself. For instance, anyone who has to carry out a series of routine inspections or adjustments can experience the familiar gap between *doing* something and *checking consciously* that he has in fact done it. That usually means that he has reached the age at which he must make the effort to work to a more conscious pattern of routine duties. He may otherwise have the disturbing sense of growing forgetful. What apparently happens in these cases is that the human mind when it has developed to a stage of considerable complexity, tends to overflow into distracting trains of thought, and thus to escape from the rigid disciplines that should be imposed upon it by the job.

It must be remembered, by the way, that, though we can describe our bodily functions with some accuracy, the workings of our mental apparatus are still very elusive. That changes do take place in them with age is fairly certain. But the manner in which these changes manifest themselves varies according to the jobs we are attempting to do. For instance, when the duties of a factory employee are under examination, it is of no help to compare them with the achievements of many elderly artists, scientists or politicians. With these latter the tendency of their modes of thought to become more diffuse may even have a positive advantage provided they are capable of co-ordinating much of this fragmented mental material into meaningful patterns. In any case they will mostly be found on inquiry to have relaxed their efforts and in reality to be working through variations upon the themes they had established some years earlier.

On the other hand, in man-machine relations the situation is quite different. The paradox of it is this—that the greater the extent to which the machine takes the work-load off a man, the more it also limits the chances he has of adapting his work methods to his age. The artist and the politician work under no such limitations. Nor, for the matter of that, was the old-time craftsman much restricted in the manipulative adjustments he was prompted to make or in the timing of his rest pauses.

When an operator on process production is simply minding or 'monitoring' an automated machine, there is even less evidence on the surface that he might be growing unreliable. For long periods of time he may be literally doing nothing at all. He may be required to keep routine records; but an employer's purpose in instructing him to do so can be merely that of occupying his mind and ensuring his continued alertness. He may often lack the stimulus given by close contact with others on the shop floor. It appears to me that in such a case the fact that would impress itself most strongly on management is the high capital cost of installations, and the losses that might result from a temporary breakdown. In precise terms, it would be felt that every operator in a department must sustain a necessary level of alertness and concentration; and there is probably as yet no criterion by which we could measure an incipient change in these qualities.

In other words, we cannot readily perceive slight deteriorations in an older man's mental functioning. We could only perceive changes in his manual performance or perhaps in his emotional state. It is to changes in his emotional state that foremen would usually appeal. They would suggest for example, that a man's interest in his work is likely to diminish, when it has become too monotonous; or again, that the motives that had compelled him to attend to his job would lose their force, once his family responsibilities lightened with the passage of time. But all this, significant as it may be in individual cases, does not touch the central problem of his continued *mental* efficiency. That often declines (as far as the demands of the job are concerned) by imperceptible degrees; and in the new technologies the net result has been to persuade management that it is advisable to adopt a pre-determined age of retirement. The age at which an older man is taken off his job is dictated at bottom by an employer's preference for being on the safe side where costly machines are involved.

Thus by something of a coincidence psychologists were emphasising the mental aspects of growing old at a time when the work-load was gradually shifting to the mind or the central nervous system. As a consequence, there was a growing suspicion that, though men age physically at very varying rates, the *mental* changes of senescence may be far more uniform in the pace of their onset.

The essence of the modern psychological theory is this—that a man's capacities for concentrated attention and decision begin to decline because of normal changes in the central nervous system. Occasionally his judgment will be seriously impaired, as in moments of physical fatigue; and it is indeed possible that we underestimate the part played by the increased fatigueability that often comes with age. Some slight muscular effort, for instance, is involved in all periods of concentration; and an older operative is not likely to escape this altogether. Nevertheless, the narrowing of the mental powers probably goes on, whether or not it is complicated by incidental fatigue.

Throughout the greater part of human history work has, of course, meant the output of muscular effort. A man's attention to the job in hand has been 'anchored' to it, as it were, by the stimulus of his own exertions. So the more the work load is shifted on to a machine, the less can he rely upon active movements to stimulate his attention. Moreover, the layout of displays and controls may become so nicely adjusted to his physical capacity, that every operation he has to perform seems as effortless as that of the machine itself. If there are deficiencies that must slowly increase with age, they lie deep within the recesses of his mental apparatus; they are affecting those complex yet apparently almost instantaneous mental functionings we identify as discrimination, judgment and the choice of appropriate responses.

One is left for the moment with two impressions:

(1) That the mental changes associated with age, while they may have had their uses socially in a primitive tribal economy, are ceasing to have any advantage under modern industrial conditions. They are a biological heritage from our remote past; but they cannot be made to harmonise with the psychologically exacting techniques of machine production.

(2) That those who direct industrial policy have necessarily been influenced by psychological theories of this kind. Many of them naturally grow sensitive about a possible deterioration in their own mental powers; and by an extension of thought they are ready to assume that their employees would also experience the psychological shortcomings of age. This is true, I think, of leading trade unionists as well as of employers. Even those, who are still apt to speak of the strain of work in terms of the muscular effort involved, are aware by this time of the importance of mental alertness. As a result, they are all becoming acclimatised to the idea that, though machinery can lighten the strain during a man's working life, it will not have the effect of prolonging that working life; on the contrary it may paradoxically tend to shorten it.

9 *The Health Status of Men of Pensionable Age*

Let us assume that the time is probably coming when most men will find themselves pensioned off somewhere around their mid sixties. A large proportion of them would then pass into the kind of *transitional phase* referred to in the O.E.C.D. Seminar on this subject.[1] For we can be sure that many of them would remain mobile and competent for a number of years. I want now to see what information we have about their general state of health. It is true that from the age of, say, 55 onwards an increasing proportion of them would have been overtaken by chronic sickness; but it is doubtful whether the proportion would ever exceed 10 per cent of the men who are 65 or so, though beyond that age the rate of increase appears to accelerate. The rest of the men who remain for their age in fairly good physical shape.

The organic changes of senescence should not be thought of as 'deteriorative'. They are only deteriorative in the sense that an older man can no longer participate in work or sport in ways that were once normal to him. In stricter definition, senescence merely means that a man is becoming slowly adapted to a more restricted and specialised set of environmental factors. Under modern conditions of manufacture and transport such specialised 'niches' of employment are ceasing to exist; that is the essence of the social dilemma.

Since about 1945 the fashion has grown up of trying to assess the level of effectiveness of men and women in successive age groups. The surveys made have introduced a few novel features, because the pioneers in this field felt it necessary to adopt yardsticks that went rather beyond the ordinary medical certificates of an individual's ailments and the length of his

[1] The term used follows the definitions quoted from the report of that Seminar in Chapter 1.

invalidity. When it came to assessing the implications of senescence it seemed imperative to use estimates that could not always be medically precise, e.g. a man's continued ability to move freely in the streets, his probable fitness to do work of some kind (if any work were available) and the prognosis that could be ventured about his health.

We have to bear in mind that there was no common agreement among all these investigators on the criteria to be adopted. The inquiries were made in diverse areas and with different motives. Nevertheless, I am inclined to accept the composite picture that emerges as representing some approximation to the facts of the case. For the most part I will confine myself to what the investigators had to say about *males* between the ages of 65 and 75 or so, i.e. the first ten years of a man's pensionable life.

Dr Sheldon's report on his Wolverhampton inquiry (1948) no doubt set the pattern for a number of subsequent surveys.[1] His sample was relatively small. There were 39 men in their late sixties and 49 in their early seventies. In effect, about 77 per cent of those aged 65–69 were judged to be physically normal for their age, and in many instances more than 'normal'; and when he came to assessing their mobility, he considered that about 74 per cent had unlimited powers of movement. Those of 70–74 appeared (again for their age) to have preserved much the same level of health; and their degree of mobility was almost as unrestricted. But, as often in such inquiries, the sample was confined to persons who were still in their own homes. Though almost 10 per cent of the men of 65–69 were housebound or bedridden, it must be assumed that several others would have succumbed to sickness by the time they were nearing 70 and would then have been found in hospitals or institutions.

[1] J. H. Sheldon, *The Social Medicine of Old Age*, Oxford University Press, 1948.

The same bias is likely to have affected the report of Drs Adams and Cheeseman[1] on their survey in Northern Ireland (1951). They admit as much themselves. The aim was to discover how far hospital attention was needed; and that limited the interviews to persons still at home. In all, 759 persons were visited.

It was taken for granted that men in the provinces outside Belfast would have been more frequently cared for in their own homes when bedridden. At all events, more than 90 per cent of those in their early sixties were competely mobile; and an even larger proportion of those in their late sixties. This does not imply that they were entirely free of sickness. But, measured by the simple test whether they could walk about at will, most of them clearly had 'no disability'.

A study of elderly persons was published by Professor Havighurst and one of his colleagues (1953); it had been carried out in a small city in mid western United States.[2] No medical examinations were made; and the assessment of health was derived from the reports of the individuals themselves, the observer's own judgment of them, and the reports given by those responsible for their care. Again the sample was very limited. Where 30 men aged 65–74 were graded according to the number of 'health problems', 24 (or about 80 per cent) had no defects or very few. As far as what was termed 'impairment of the legs' is concerned, it appears that the majority of all persons aged 65–74 (male and female) were considered normal. In precise figures 71 per cent of 64 persons fell into this group. The larger proportion of defects among the older women tipped the scale a little below what it would be for men alone.

In a socio-medical survey of old persons living at home in Dorset (1954), Drs Simonds and Stewart graded their state of health on the basis of reports from practitioners and of their

[1] G. F. Adams and E. A. Cheeseman, *Old People in North Ireland; Report to the Northern Ireland Hospitals Authority*, 1951.

[2] Robert J. Havighurst and Ruth Albrecht, *Older People*, Longmans, Green & Co., 1953.

own impressions in the course of interviews.[1] There were 53 men in their sixties. Only about 10 per cent of them had very restricted powers of movement or were at the time confined to bed. The remainder had few or no defects, or at least 'seemed fit at the time of the interview'. When it came to a prognosis of their likely state of health, it was felt that 66 per cent of them would probably remain fit for some time.

The sample of men in their seventies was larger (94); almost a quarter of them had restricted mobility; but it was felt that more than 40 per cent of the whole age group were likely to remain for their age in reasonably good health. It must be remembered, of course, that here again the men were still living in their own homes; the figures give no indication of the amount of hospitalisation among men of the same ages.

The Sheffield study made by Professor Hobson and Dr Pemberton[2] was published in 1955. Quantitative assessments were carried out of the degrees of physical disablement experienced by older persons selected from a previous survey. There were 38 men in their sample aged 65–69; and it was judged that of these about 81 per cent had unrestricted mobility. The writers comment, however, that it would be a mistake to assume that all these 'unrestricted' men were fit and well. It was simply a refusal to give in to the aches and infirmities of age, that allowed many still to be classified as *mobility unrestricted*. The causes of partial immobility were mainly cardiovascular disease, joint conditions and bronchitis. The writers show incidentally that the men's own self-assessments of their fitness was higher than the assessments made by physicians; it was assumed that people are more apt to allow for age, when judging of the degree of fitness they can claim to enjoy.

Dr Richardson's inquiries in Aberdeen (1956) covered 111

[1] W. H. Simonds and Alice Stewart, 'Old People Living in Dorset', *British Journal of Preventive Medicine*, October 1954.

[2] W. Hobson and J. Pemberton, *The Health of the Elderly at Home*, Butterworth & Co. Ltd., 1955.

men aged 65–69[1]; apparently they were all retired. Since a fair proportion of those approached for interview could not be visited, it must be presumed that several such men were among the less fit. Dr Richardson was concerned to assess their probable capacity for work of some kind; and he depended upon their own statements, their past health histories, the frequency of medical attendance, and the presence of any defect or complaint. He concluded that of the 111 men of these ages about 42 per cent would have been fit for any job and a further 38 per cent would have needed some selection of suitable work. 19 per cent had disabilities that would have made further work unlikely. Of course, when men have been retired for three or four years, their fitness to resume work is not easy to assess; but it at least appears that about 80 per cent of the men conveyed an impression of tolerably good health.

In the reports of their Birmingham inquiries (1958) Professor McKeown and his colleagues attempt, among other things, to make the same kind of assessment as that in the work of Dr Richardson.[2] But the numbers were larger (458 men aged 65–69); and their method was different. The cooperation of eleven medical practitioners had been elicited; and it was thought that the uniformity and the competence of diagnosis would thus be ensured. In the outcome, 14 per cent of the men of these ages were held to be unfit for employment; 11·6 per cent were considered no longer fit for their original employment but capable of some other job. The proportion of men held unfit for work increased slowly from the age of 65 upwards; and at 69 it rose more steeply, i.e. from about one in ten to about one in four. However, more than a third of the 458 men were no longer working; and the same criticism applies to this mode of assessment as to that used in Aberdeen. But there is little doubt that about 85 per cent of the men gave the

[1] I. M. Richardson. 'Retirement: A Socio-Medical Study.' *Scottish Medical Journal*, 1956.

[2] R. G. Brown, T. McKeown and A. G. W. Whitfield, 'Observations on the Medical Condition of Men in the Seventh Decade, II. Fitness for Employment', *British Medical Journal*, 1958, I, 558.

impression of still being capable of work of some kind; it does not follow that so large a proportion could really have remained employable, as matched with the demands of modern industry.

The report on the United States National Health Survey of 1957–8 (1959) is more comprehensive.[1] The percentages published were based on the total population outside institutions, whether the individuals concerned had or had not any chronic conditions. The material was derived from household interviews; and the inquiries covered about 150,000 persons of all ages. When 'mobility' was used as a criterion, it refers to a man's capacity for moving about freely, partially or not at all; 'activity' is taken to mean the range of activity of persons who were or had been working normally. Presumably retired men were classified as relatively active 'for their age'.

As for 'mobility', some 89 per cent of the men aged 65–74 were held to be either uninhibited or to find their physical complaints did not limit their movements. But only 60·4 per cent of the same men were so well placed in regard to their 'activity'; a quarter of them were partially limited in that respect by chronic conditions, and 14·5 per cent were classed as suffering from a major limitation.

Professor van Zonneveld directed an extensive health survey in the Netherlands; it closed in 1957 and was published in 1961.[2] The intention was to have it carried out by the elderly persons' own practitioners—more or less along the lines of health insurance examinations (as had been the inquiry made by Professor McKeown). There were, however, sampling difficulties and some delays before the work could be completed. In their approach to the general physical condition of those examined, physicians were simply asked, 'What is the general physical impression the person makes on you?'

By this standard the men of 65–69 years (350) were judged in

[1] *Health Statistics—from the U.S. National Health Survey* (Limitation of Activity and Mobility due to Chronic Conditions) U.S. Department of Health, Education and Welfare, 1959.

[2] R. J. van Zonneveld, *The Health of the Aged*, Van Gorcum—Assem, Netherlands, 1961.

82 per cent of cases to be in 'good' physical condition; the proportion of those aged 70–74 was much the same. The method of research seems to have been a reliable one in the sense that most of the practitioners would have been trained in the same diagnostic procedures; if there was some selective bias, it was probably slight. In most of such surveys there would be an unavoidable tendency to judge elderly persons as fit 'for their age'.

The work under the direction of Mrs Cole and her colleague covered selected areas of the United Kingdom and relied on samples drawn from the electoral register.[1] It was carried out in 1959–60 and the Report was published in 1962. The inquiry was concerned with the economic circumstances of the elderly; but it also touched upon their relative mobility. No clinical assessments were made; and the writers admit that, even where mobility was in question, an element of subjective judgment probably entered in. Out of 60 men aged 65–69 about 93·3 per cent were held to have an unrestricted mobility; the remaining 6·7 per cent only moved with effort, at all events out of doors. There were 33 men aged 70–74; and of these 87·9 per cent were equally unrestricted for their age, 3·0 per cent were partly restricted and 9·1 per cent were housebound.

After a lay survey of elderly persons had been carried out in Swansea, medical examinations were made by Dr Parsons in 1961.[2] It was felt in the outcome that the definitions of 'mobility' differed as between the lay and the medical assessments. In the case of the lay inquiry the men aged 65–74 were classified by their capacity for movement. 87·2 per cent were considered to have unrestricted mobility, 7·0 to be restricted outside the home and 5·8 per cent to be housebound or bedridden. In the final medical sample the age groups were more narrowly divided. In effect Dr. Parsons held that about 76 per cent of his 34 men aged 65–69 were in good or average health; the

[1] Dorothy Cole with J. R. G. Utting, *Economic Circumstances of Old People*, The Codicote Press, 1962.

[2] P. L. Parsons, 'The Health of Swansea's Old Folk'. Unpublished (1964).

remaining 24 per cent were in poor, though not necessarily a very poor, condition. Of the 40 men aged 70–74 about 27 per cent were in poor or very poor health. As for their mobility, he judged that about 26 per cent of all the men of 65–74 were to some extent affected by such conditions as dyspnoea, frailty, lassitude and arthritis; a proportion of these forms of impairment would no doubt have been overlooked by lay interviewers.

Allowing for wide variations in the criteria that were applied, we can say that about four out of five of the men in their late sixties gave the impression of being thoroughly mobile and alert in mind. I have shown reasons for qualifying some of the statements made; for instance, the relative ages of the men must have affected the opinions expressed by most of the observers. But it is plain, I think, that the age span 65–75 constitutes the essence of the new social problem with which we are now faced. It emerges as a kind of *intermediate* phase in human life the men concerned can no longer perhaps continue in their normal employment, yet most of them are still far from being infirm.

This is an aspect of the ageing process to which little regard has been paid. Until it was forced upon our attention by the trend of industrial policy, it seemed of minor significance. But it has become clear that we need to know a good deal more about its characteristic attitudes and the social opportunities that are still open to it.

10 *The Social Problems Implicit in a Policy of Retirement*

The main problem can be simply stated. Most men will be retired from gainful work with a reserve of energies they can still call upon; and a proportion of them (whatever that proportion may be) will never remain psychologically contented, unless those energies find an appropriate outlet. With the residue, who have no restless disposition, we need not concern ourselves; presumably they will settle down at ease to their retirement.

Now, we know that for most economists this problem has little interest, since by definition such men would no longer be producing goods or services. They are significant only as part of total consumption. Moreover, they no longer fall within the proper responsibilities of employers and trade unions; for the function of all these latter, as I have pointed out, lies with the men who are actually at work or held to be employable. Whose duty will it be in that case to satisfy the temperamental demands of the reluctant pensioner?

Two questions will here be asked. (1) What do we know of the attitudes of manual workers about retirement? (2) What efforts are being made by Society to find a continued outlet for their energies?

Attitudes to Retirement

We need not elaborate the reasons why some men want to remain active in the *post-employment* stage of their lives. But it is relevant to quote again from the Slough Report mentioned in an earlier chapter.[1] Interviews were held with 507 manual workers, still in employment, from the age of 55 upwards.

[1] Chapter 4 (*Workers Nearing Retirement*, The Nuffield Foundation. 1963).

'Though money was an important reason for continuing at work, it seems rarely to be the sole or dominant reason. Only a quarter of the men interviewed af all ages felt that financial reasons would compel them to remain or had done so in the past. Few of the personnel officers were apparently aware of this; for the majority of them were sure that men only continued to work after 65 for the pay packet. It should here be recognised that, when older men apply for a job or ask to be retained, they tend to emphasise their income problems. It is an objective argument; distrust of leisure or fear of being cut off from the working community do not seem to them to be good reasons to put forward when approaching an employer for work.' I am inclined to think that the underlying motive is often an urge to prolong the disciplined habits of daily life, that are associated with the demands of a job. The majority of men would have been acclimatised to such habits since their early schooling; and many of them have a sense that they will be lost in the unfamiliar element of complete leisure. They may wish their hours of work to be limited; but there is a distinction between limited hours and no ordered rhythm of work at all. Apparently there have been few attempts to discover what are the retrospective views of men *after* their retirement. This would be a more sensible procedure than the commoner practice of asking them their intentions *in advance*; for their intentions at such a time are often vague and vacillating. But Dr Alastair Weir has reported interviews with 50 men fairly soon after their withdrawal from work.[1] These were Glasgow manual workers, who all belonged to clubs and were in other respects a well-adjusted group. They were asked what advice they would give to someone at work who was shortly to retire. More than a quarter of them advised not giving up work at all, if that were possible; and over a third counselled the pursuit of some kind of activity, interest or hobby.

Where men in a pre-retirement stage have been asked their

[1] Unpublished Report submitted to the Glasgow Retirement Council, on 'Inquiry into Attitudes to Retirement', 1961.

intentions, the numbers who express a wish to go on working seem usually to vary with their age, i.e. with the relative remoteness of the event. The numbers certainly do not correspond with the efforts they subsequently make to continue at work. Moreover, I do not think that the proportion of retired men, who cancel their pension and temporarily return to full-time work, is ever large.

In the years 1961–3 the average number of male pensioners who yearly adopted that course of action was not much over a thousand.[1] There is no record of the periods that had elapsed since they first went into retirement; but inquiries suggest that the periods rarely exceed six months. In other words, these were exceptional cases; an opportunity of further employment had come before the habit of work had lost its hold upon them. Most men, however buoyant their original intentions, are probably discouraged in seeking further work by the apparent scarcity of alternative jobs.

In the years following 1951, a study was made of men approaching their retirement in a Liverpool manufacturing firm, that had adopted a fixed retiring age for all its employees.[2] The views of 171 men were obtained. About 68 per cent said they wanted to continue, the majority for as long as they felt able to do so. A little over half of the 171 would have liked to remain with the firm, either on their normal work or on a lighter job. The main reason advanced was a decline in income; but an apprehension of boredom and loneliness was evidently felt by at least some of them. Miss Pearson quotes one comment 'Work keeps you fit and occupies the mind. In any case I'd miss the other men so much if I retired'.

This sense of the importance of *active* work was mentioned also in the Slough Report cited above. 'They were all manual workers. They might want an occupation that demanded less physical effort; but that did not imply a need for sedentary

[1] The average annual number of new male claimants in the same three years was about 203,100.

[2] Margaret Pearson, 'Transition from Work to Retirement', *Occupational Psychology*, April 1957, Vol. 31.

pursuits and certainly not for intellectual ones. They made it very clear that in their view, if the mind is to be occupied, the body must be occupied as well . . . It is possible that for many ageing manual workers an abrupt cessation of physical activities is as deleterious as would be sudden bouts of strenuous exercise for an ageing sedentary worker. Certainly the men interviewed seemed convinced that this was the case . . . Physical activities were associated in their thoughts with the preservation of their peace of mind.'

In a survey published in 1956 Drs Ferguson Anderson and Nairn Cowan recorded the attitudes of men over 65 at a consultative health centre near Glasgow.[1] It appears that of 323 men (some still working) about 89 per cent believed that retirement is detrimental to the health and well-being of older men. 'The reasons for this overwhelming dislike of enforced retirement . . . were primarily financial and the need for older men to do something tangibly useful to give a meaning to their lives'. Among the 323 men 108 had had direct experience of compulsory retirement; some 30 of them had for a time at least secured another job. Almost all of them expressed resentment at the implied limits to their freedom of employment. Thus the opinions were here mainly retrospective; but it may be doubted whether the attitudes they then displayed would in any case have told us precisely how many men might in fact have continued to work if they had the chance.

I am disposed to think that we should get a more realistic picture of men's attitudes, if we knew what happens when they are offered a chance of part-time employment immediately on being retired. A few firms have opened special workshops for this purpose. Communications from three of these, situated in the South East, the West Midlands and Scotland, suggest that the numbers normally accepting the offer lie between a quarter and a third of all current retirements. Some of those who refuse the offer may, of course, be in poor physical condition;

[1] W. Ferguson Anderson and Nairn R. Cowan, 'Work and Retirement', *Lancet*, December 29, 1956.

and others may be intending to look for work elsewhere. But though there is a measure of agreement in the estimates, such proportions cannot be taken as constant; attitudes could change rapidly, if it were generally known that part-time work was immediately available. Let us simply assume for the moment that about 30 per cent of men, when faced with retirement, would welcome the chance of a fairly prolonged 'tapering off' period of active work.

Some of the comments I have quoted imply a judgment on the mental well-being of such men. It would be difficult, however, to prove statistically that it is inadvisable for any men to leave the ordered routine of work. Does their health ever deteriorate for that cause alone? The objection could be raised that, since large numbers of men plainly adapt themselves to a state of complete retirement, those who do not might in any case have always been more liable to moods of anxiety or depression. We are still in the negative realm rather of opinions than of medical evidence. But that does not mean that the opinions are without substance. On the positive side the psychological argument for continued work has been cautiously summarised by a medical journal in an issue mainly devoted to the problems of age.[1] They ran as follows:

1. It is usually good that a man should continue to exercise his mind and muscles on tasks that lie within his experience and his competence.

2. It maintains his *morale* to find that he can achieve results that will absorb part of his interests and give him an emotional satisfaction.

3. It is helpful when a man can preserve his sense of self-esteem by carrying out work with which he may socially identify his status.

4. It is probably good for a man to continue in the companionship of other men who are engaged with him on productive work of some kind.

[1], 'The Importance for Ageing Men of Some Continuity in Work Habits' *Public Health*, Vol. LXXII, September 1958.

Let us abide by our hypothesis that about 30 per cent of manual workers are very conscious on retirement of some or all of these positive needs. We know that many of them would not have prepared their minds or modes of life for the abrupt transition; they would have trusted at best that chance would somehow throw an occupation in their way when they felt a lack of it. Even if they have given any thought at all to the matter, for what active pursuit or occupation *would* they prepare themselves? What semblance of continued work can the modern world offer them?

It is unnecessary to be exhaustive under these headings. But it does seem necessary to analyse out the implications of some of them.

Plans for prolonging the pattern of a Working Life

The remainder of this chapter will be given over to a critical review of such methods as have been so far suggested for dealing with the human problem. Most of them have already been tried, however experimentally. I am assuming, of course, that all prolongation of work rhythms must henceforth be looked for *outside a man's normal place of work*. There seem to have been five methods attempted.

(1) The employment of retired men on 'out-work' contracts, negotiated with various manufacturing firms.

(2) The direct employment of such men by industrial firms in sheltered workshops.

(3) The arrangement with various institutions, etc., for small equipment and other requisites to be produced for them by groups of retired men.

(4) The systematic planning in the community of various kinds of domestic repair and servicing jobs, on the assumption that many of them could be carried out in an organised way by retired men.

(5) The recruitment of retired men for voluntary work

(with a guarantee of expenses) in the Health and Welfare Services, etc.

(1) *Outwork.* The idea that manual workers, on being retired from their normal employment, might undertake various forms of 'out-work' or 'home-work' seems peculiar to the United Kingdom. There are reasons, however, for thinking that the opportunities will be limited; and it is as well to get the whole matter into perspective.

Out-work and home-work are largely survivals from an industrial past. The two terms are not quite synonymous. Out-work is more inclusive; for it may mean that the jobs are being carried out by small sub-contractors, who employ a few workers on specific operations. But in both cases materials and partly finished work are conveyed or delivered from a factory or main workshop. The jobs are then completed at a contract price, and usually on a piece-work basis. Most of the work is geographically localised; and in large measure it now meets the requirements of the clothing and allied industries. About 80 per cent of all out-work still done in Leicester, for example, Luton and Northampton falls into this category; and women, especially married women, predominate.

It seems probable, though the evidence is not quite conclusive, that the demand for 'out-workers' is steadily declining; or it may be that women are less interested than they once were in this source of income. At all events, the Health Departments of the Local Authorities inspect premises in which home-work and out-work is carried on; and they are provided by employers with lists of out-workers. Since this information is summarised annually in the reports published by Medical Officers of Health, we have some chance of observing the trends. It would be impossible to say whether the statistics are strictly comparable from year to year. But to start with, I have examined a sample of London health reports.

In the year 1931, six of the Boroughs of East London

(Bethnal Green, Hackney, Poplar, Shoreditch, Stepney and Stoke Newington) had among them an aggregate of 7,008 out-workers; about 62 per cent of these were working for the clothing and allied trades. By 1961 the numbers had declined to 2,837, i.e. to about 40 per cent of the 1931 level.

To check this apparent trend I took a group of Boroughs elsewhere in London (Camberwell, Lambeth, Paddington, St Marylebone, Southwark, Wandsworth and Westminster). Here the aggregate decline over the same period in the number of out-workers was from 5,508 to 3,361, i.e. a fall to 60 per cent of the 1931 level; and it must be noted that in 1961 more than four-fifths of the total demand came from the clothing industries —mostly no doubt undertaken by women.

Meanwhile communications received from a few of the old-established centres of out-work seem to confirm this trend. In Yeovil indeed, according to the Chamber of Trade, glove-making is still largely a home industry. But in Nottingham out-work appears to be almost entirely limited to lace-making; and in that industry too mechanisation is advancing steadily. In Northampton, again, out-work on the hand-sewing of foot-wear is stated to be declining; 'It will hardly exist in five years' time'.

We must recognise moreover that there is today a good deal of competition for the relatively small amount of outwork still available. The authorities responsible for mental hospitals, prisons, the welfare of the blind and partly disabled, etc., are all showing an interest in securing industrial contracts of a similar kind. Their motives are plain; it is felt that such a tenuous association with the world of industry could have a normalising, therapeutic or stimulating effect on those who are entrusted to their care. An examination of the types of out-work contracts some of these institutions have managed to negotiate throws a little light on the whole subject.

In the mid 'fifties the mental hospitals began to study seriously the chances of forming a *liaison* with local industries. By 1961 about 46 per cent of hospitals for the mentally subnormal and about 64 per cent of hospitals for the mentally sick had obtained contracts. They are well aware of the importance of guaranteeing prompt delivery; and in many instances they have appointed officers to superintend their workshops and to maintain a close relationship with manufacturing firms. It is evident indeed, that they are already establishing a kind of priority right for any out-work jobs that happen to be available.

In 1960 the Ministry of Health asked for returns from a number of mental hospitals, that reported the existence of industrial schemes. By the Ministry's permission I have analysed these returns. There were in all 80 records. The items they give will show concisely the nature of out-work today (apart from that done by the clothing and similar trades). The 80 hospitals made 181 references to current contracts; several of them, of course, had more than one.

Table XI

ANALYSIS OF 181 OUT-WORK CONTRACTS SECURED BY MENTAL HOSPITALS IN 1960

Description of the out-work	*Number of references*
Assembling card-board cartons (or paper and polythene bags)	38
Dismantling Post Office equipment (mainly telephones and meters)	26
Packing (small engineering components, toys, fancy goods, paint, etc.)	29
Assembling (fancy goods, toys, small domestic and other utensils)	28
Assembling (light engineering and electrical components, parts of TV. sets, etc.)	21
Salvaging and sorting of scrap metal, dismantling bottle tops, tops, repairing crates, etc.	13
Making, trimming and painting of plastic mouldings (mainly toys and small utensils)	13
Miscellaneous (light clothing, onion peeling, small concrete fabrications, etc.)	13

Clearly the range of out-work is limited and is associated with a few of the more specialised branches of manufacture. It is very unevenly distributed. The main problem facing the mental hospitals has been that of maintaining continuity. Thirteen of them mentioned the need to keep up pressure on sympathetic employers. In general, while 42 of the hospitals stated that a continuity of work had on the whole been maintained, 35 testified that the flow had been fluctuating or unreliable. The most frustrating problem of all was probably the shortage in some Regions of suitable industries; at the time of the inquiry Wales and the South West seem to have been the least favourably placed. Some of the more successful hospitals apparently thought their only safe course would be to enlarge their empires; and a few of these were conscious of the risk of setting up an inter-hospital competition.

It is in this already crowded market that workshops for retired persons are trying to secure a foothold. They are usually referred to as workrooms for the elderly; and, as a matter of fact, the average age of participants seems to be over 70. About two out of three of them are women who tend to represent a somewhat younger element than the men. Workrooms have been opening since 1951; and there are now about 60 of them (more than half in London and the South East). The hours worked are limited; and the aim has evidently been less that of providing work than of maintaining mental health and stability

The initiative and financial support have mainly come from voluntary bodies, either directly or through a sponsoring committee. Some Local Authorities, however, are also involved; and a few of these latter have taken advantage of an interpretation of a Ministry of Health circular to make themselves entirely responsible for a workroom.[1]

To summarise the present state of affairs—no one would seek to discourage a plan for securing local 'out-work' in the interests of a few elderly persons. But it must be appreciated

[1] Circular 12/62, Para. 10. The Minister . . . is advised that 'recreation' in Section 31 of the National Assistance Act does not exclude 'work centres' or 'occupational centres', where elderly people are able incidentally to earn small sums of money by making goods for sale or by doing out-work for local firms and factories, provided that production and earnings are only ancillary to the main purpose of the centre, namely, to keep elderly people fit and active . . .

that the method has a very limited potential. Much of the work carried out in the existing workrooms is probably best done by such elderly women as had acquired an aptitude for it. Besides, mental hospitals, workshops for the blind and other welfare institutions have by this time pre-empted a large proportion of the goodwill of industrial employers. It is not advisable to look to out-work contracts as a reliable way of helping ex-employees to prolong their working lives for a further term of years.

(2) *Sheltered Industrial Workshops.* Very few of these have been yet recorded. At least three methods are known to exist:

(a) That of employing a small number of the firm's pensioners for limited hours (e.g. in evening shifts) on work that would normally be part of the production process. Such jobs as light packing are suitable for the purpose. The motives are largely philanthropic; and since the work is probably done at a restrained pace, the workshop on a strictly costed basis is not likely to be viable. The plan will not have a wide appeal among employers.

(b) That of employing some of a firm's pensioners to fabricate special products; such products might either be marketed or utilized by the firm itself in lieu of accessories that it would otherwise have purchased in the open market. Thus a manufacturing concern in the Netherlands sponsors a workshop in which a few of its pensioners turn out models of machines for sale to university departments, museums, etc. In this and similar experiments much has obviously depended on the choice of an organiser for designing models, initiating ex-craftsmen into the work and expanding the market. There seems no reason why an employer, if he wishes to do so, should not plan to have commodities produced in this way, and that in a workshop subsidiary to his main plant. But in so far as the work demands skill and adaptability, it might not be appropriate for the main run of older operatives; only where fairly simple machine processes were involved, would semi-skilled men be proportionately represented in the workshop. At that stage it would become difficult to distinguish between the workshop products and those of normal manufacture; the scheme would necessarily be of dubious economic value. Impressive as are two or three of the established workshops, they can scarcely be reckoned as more than inspired prototypes; and so far they have not been widely imitated.

(c) That of employing some of a firm's pensioners on such work as scrap recovery, the light repair of tools and accessories, and other operations of the kind that were referred to in an earlier chapter as 'nuisance jobs'. This method has only been adopted so far in two or three firms; but it might ultimately prove to be the basic pattern. It is more likely to approximate to an economic proposition. Its usefulness clearly depends, however, on the characteristics of an undertaking, e.g. on the amount and type of scrap metal that is evolved, and on the extent to which it appears worth while to salvage and repair tools, accessories, fitments and so on. No doubt it is always possible to repair containers, protective clothing, goggles and other items in common use; that is a matter for managerial decisions.

Certainly there are firms that have had steel scrap fabricated into useful fitments by employing a few of their pensioners on obsolete machines. But that might only be practicable in a small number of engineering plants. To apply a similar plan to, e.g. a chemical plant might be very difficult. Thus the principle becomes increasingly questionable as we move to manufacturing firms that have little or no scrap to be disposed of.

The argument for thinking in terms of such a pensioner workshop is this. There must always remain in a plant a number of those relatively unprofitable and incidental tasks, that are usually classed as salvaging and 'nuisance' jobs. They may be of minor importance to production; but they are essential. In theory, then, there could be some advantage in having a reserve of labour composed of a few elderly ex-employees, paid on a piece work basis and employed for two or three days a week. It will have been noticed, by the way, that a fairly large proportion of the jobs committed to the mental hospitals consisted of the dismantling of light equipment and the salvaging of scrap. There is possibly more of this in the aggregate than we realise; and we should not dismiss out of hand the theory that industry could be so reorganised as to pass over an amount of this to self-supervised workshops of retired operatives.

It was upon information obtained in a few of the industrial workshops that I based my estimate that perhaps 30 per cent of manual workers are at present interested in prolonging work beyond the age of retirement. The methods adopted by the industries have, however, too many variables in them to allow of a discussion of their general use. There may not be as yet more than a dozen workshops of the kind in the U.K. or more than one or two in either France or the Netherlands. Furthermore, the numbers employed in them are comparatively small. It can hardly be questioned that the plan will have to show it pays its way, before it can hope to gain wider adherence in industry.

(3) *Work for Institutions.* There are so few cases where an institution obtains small requisites, apparently on a continuous basis, from organised groups of pensioners, that this method can be soon dismissed. Occasionally orders have been given to workrooms for wooden shapes used in the rehabilitation of limbs, for collecting money-boxes, etc. But these were needed only in minute numbers. One example of a fairly settled arrangement comes from Michigan, U.S.A.[1] Wooden toys, etc., are made for children's hospital wards. Designs are supplied to a pensioners' club; and most of the costs of material seem to have been met by the pensioners themselves. There is no

[1] *Ageing.* U.S. Department of Health, Education and Welfare, October, 1963.

inherent reason, however, why this initiative should not be expanded. For instance, the making of plastic toys, souvenirs, etc., is a relatively simple operation, once the equipment has been installed.

(4) *Household Servicing and Repairs*. Since it is recognised that indeterminate numbers of pensioners do in fact already find occasional or seasonal work for householders on gardening, re-decorating, minor repairs, etc., it has seemed reasonable to suggest that this could be carried much further. There is, of course, a set of unknown factors in the equation. Are there householders who would be glad to avail themselves of such services, if they were only informed where to obtain them? Are there pensioners who have such services to offer, if they only knew to whom they might apply? The theory is strengthened a little by the evidence that, where an individual has set himself up locally as a kind of private exchange, he has succeeded in several cases in matching a potential demand with a potential supply. The natural inference is that there must be a good deal of unsatisfied demand; householders who can afford them need services that are no longer obtainable through the traditional channels. It has been argued that, if the method could be experimentally systematised in some of the local offices of the Ministry of Labour, an unexpected amount of success might follow.

Writers on both sides of the Atlantic, who seek to advise on profitable activities in retirement, probably rely most on servicing jobs. They mention, for instance, the repair of furniture or china, the servicing of household garments, minor electrical or mechanical adjustments, etc. It is assumed that pensioners would have in some way gained the necessary skills. The principle needs, however, one or two qualifications. Let us suppose that an increasing number of *employed* families can now afford to use services that were formerly the privilege of a few. Gardening or re-decoration services might be welcome to such families; but we should have to inquire whether the repair of domestic furniture, etc., still seems to them preferable to the simpler process of replacing them as obsolescent.

A more serious problem is the usual one, that pensioners might in these cases be up against competition in a limited market. The subject has already been mentioned (Chapter 3). Young employed men are frequently prepared to contract with householders for carrying out most of the jobs in their spare time; it has become for many of them a part of their own domestic budgeting. Since it would be administratively impossible to reserve some types of work for pensioners alone, the success of an effort to systematise their gainful activities must remain doubtful.

(5) *Voluntary Social Work.* One of the methods most commonly advocated is that of attracting newly retired men (usually on a voluntary basis) into Health and Welfare Services and the like. Such men are already attracted in sufficient numbers to support the idea that the habit might easily spread. The Social Services may be described in this context as an organised effort to fill gaps left in the personal service, that is rendered to those in need by their families or near neighbours. The Social Services are probably due for a systematic overhaul and expansion; and for the most part they will concentrate upon problems of mental sub-normality, delinquency, physical immobility and housebound old age.

Here too there is likely to be some competition, even in the voluntary field. If we assume that social work becomes increasingly popular, it will not be the retired alone who are prompted to take it up. Young men and women, and middle-aged housewives, are all being urged to see in it an outlet for their spare energies. We may, in fact, come to realise that it is advisable to partition out the ground.

Perhaps the most useful suggestion so far is that which would see a certain identity of interests among all persons aged over, say, 65 or 67. They comprise, of course, a wide range of physical conditions and states of health. But in simple terms, a man of 67, who is in the regular habit of visiting and assisting one or two elderly housebound men of 80 or so, may reckon that in ten years' time he might well need similar attentions. A short course of training would probably enable many retired men to play an important part in this branch of the Health and Welfare Services.

At all events, there are indications that a few industries are already trying to encourage this kind of activity among their ex-employees. For instance, two large undertakings, both with a fairly rigid retiring age, plan for recently retired men to report back, so far as practicable, on the domestic well-being of their older colleagues. Expenses are met from the Welfare Departments, to which reports can be passed for attention. The same principle has been recognised by some of the larger Trade Unions in the U.S.A., though they have apparently not yet adopted any organised plan of activities.

If anyone wants to pursue this side of the inquiry, he would first, I think, have to study two or three preliminary problems. To begin with, there is the matter of competition, to which I have already referred; the voluntary social services are not going to remain permanently undermanned. Then there is the question of the real extent to which such services are needed by members of the community. The unsatisfied demand is still large; but it is certainly not unlimited. The numbers of households that are effectively self-supporting, or can at least rely at need on a few neighbours, must far exceed the numbers that have to look for assistance to the Welfare Services. But the essence of the matter, no doubt, is this; if a man's retirement is to mean to him a choice between voluntary activities and no planned activities at all, then we should inquire what factors bias him in the choice he makes. If the main factor appears to be a financial one, we might feel impelled by that discovery alone to re-examine our general theory of pensions and incomes.

All these schemes are still merely experimental; they are at best 'model' schemes, that have never managed to work loose from a pilot stage and exert a wider influence on social policy. In the development of some of them a great deal of care and thought has been expended; they have had well deserved publicity. Yet they still remain isolated schemes. We cannot but suspect that in most cases there are limiting factors at work. The methods are probably suited only to very specialised industrial or social conditions; and they are thus unable to provide a comprehensive outlet for the energies of retired workers.

Little has been said about the kinds of alternative employment that pensioners occasionally take up (usually on their own initiative) quite outside what had been their normal places of work. This is due to the lack of any firm statistical evidence; we are still depending largely on generalities based on a few individual cases. However, the 1961 Census Tables do throw a little light, if not on the total volume of such employment, at least on the main forms it apparently takes. One Table shows how many men, following the instructions of the Census, had indicated that they were at the moment only on 'part-time work'.[1] Now, we can assume that most pensioners in their late sixties, if they are inclined to get a job, would seek part-time employment; that would enable them to keep more or less within the limits imposed by the earnings rule. While we have no means of discovering whether part-time employees in this age group are in fact all on a State pension, we may take it from what is known of their ways of thought, that the large majority of them would certainly have become pensioners. Why deny oneself the support of a state pension when one is plainly launched henceforth upon a rather precarious labour market?

We will avoid any detailed analysis of the Census figures and confine the inquiry to the age group 65–69. The Table gives 53,960 men of those ages as employed part-time in 1961. The numbers are likely to be an understatement. On the assumption

[1] 1961 Census (England and Wales). Occupational Tables, Table 14.

that almost all of them were technically 'retired', they would represent less than 10 per cent of all retired men of the same ages. Some pensioners might have had good reason for not admitting that they were still in employment; and some, whose work tended to be seasonal or spasmodic, might not have been working at all at the time of the Census. The actual jobs on which they were engaged are another matter; there are grounds for supposing that they provide a very fair sample of the types of occupation that would still be open to an able-bodied pensioner. They show us where part-time work is most likely to be available.

To begin with, in many branches of manufacture and transport the opportunities of part-time work are plainly negligible —though in a few industries (e.g. printing, wood products and clothing) somewhere round 10 per cent of such employed older men stated that their hours were limited. This is probably because numerous small firms in the industries have some need of occasional 'stand-in' operatives. But there is a group of occupations, in which the proportion of part-time workers looks unusually high among the employed men of similar ages. Table XII shows what percentages of the employed men of 65–69 years claimed to be on part-time work in these occupations. Among them they comprise about 60 per cent of all the

Table XII

PERCENTAGES OF EMPLOYED MEN IN THE AGE GROUP 65–69 WHO WERE RECORDED AS ONLY ON PART-TIME WORK (1961)

Occupation	*Per cent working Part-time*	*Occupation*	*Per cent working Part-time*
Farm workers	35·4	Clerical workers	21·3
Gardeners	44·9	Doorkeepers, Watchmen, etc.	37·4
Building workers	19·6	Caretakers	35·7
Storemen, etc.	15·3	Office cleaners, etc.	56·3
Employed on unspecific 'Labouring' work	16·8	Employed on various jobs in welfare, sport and recreation	23·0

part-time workers in that age group; so we have some reason for surmising that it is precisely to jobs of this kind that pensioners tend as a rule to gravitate.

We must remember that the numbers involved were in no case very large; and some of the men, such as caretakers and storemen are likely to have been on 'stand-in' jobs. The highest numbers were those of the clerical workers and the men whose 'labouring' duties were not precisely specified. As for the overall chances of finding part-time employment once a man is past 65, it seems that about 21 per cent of such older employed men *of all ages* had managed to limit their hours of work. The subject, of course, is worth further study, because any attempt to widen the field in the interest of pensioners would presumably have to operate along these lines.

But we must dismiss the belief that a retired man could always find an alternative job, if only he had the will. We have to see the active-minded, able-bodied and reluctant pensioner as essentially a product of our own times. Nor is his situation peculiar to the West alone. The situation will be the same wherever a country's economy enters the same stage of its industrial evolution; for it is implicit in the industrial and social laws of technological progress.

A Commentary on United States Experience

The only sound reason for referring briefly to another industrial country is to bring into relief a few contrasts. I shall consider no more than three elements in the complex American scene.

1. Changes that had taken place in the rates of retirement between the U.S. Census Years 1950 and 1960.

2. Distinctive roles adopted by the Trade Unions in face of their own retirement problem.

3. Some contributions made by American sociologists to a better understanding of changes in men's personal attitude likely to accompany the withdrawal from normal employment.

The image I give will necessarily be lacking in depth and substance.

1. *U.S. Statistical Evidence on Retirement*

'By 1960', has written one American economist, 'the preponderant majority of the wage and salary workers in the U.S.A. had become part of the conventional pattern of retirement'.[1] He took as a basis the U.S. Census Years 1950 and 1960. In effect, the proportion of men who continued in the labour force beyond the age of 65 had declined in marked degree. The changes in 'worker rates' can be summarised thus for individual years of life:

Years	*65*	*69*	*75*
1950	70·3	54·5	33·9
1960	56·3	39·2	26·2

[1] Seymour L. Wolfbein (U.S. Department of Labour, Manpower Administration), 'Changing Patterns of Working Life'. Paper submitted to an International Gerontological Seminar, 1963.

The declines are not dissimilar from our own. It is significant, however, that the declines in the U.S.A. probably began to accelerate a little earlier—and that there are indications that the accepted age of withdrawal is now moving down into the early sixties. In 1950 about 11·7 per cent of men were already retired by the time they were passing into age 65. If we allow that some of this may have been due to invalidity, the U.K. was then in much the same position. But in 1960 the rate of retirements by the same age had become in America no less than 29·0 per cent. 'The sixty-fifth year of life has now become the truly conventional age of retirement in the U.S.A. The rate of retirement between ages 64 and 65 tripled from 1950 to 1960'.

In consequence, there has been a parallel growth of the number of years spent in retirement. If we take the *average* man of 60 (i.e. allowing for mortality and for the fact that some men go on working well beyond 65), we are told that in 1900 such a man could expect about 2·8 years in retirement; by 1960 he could expect about 7·3 years. For many, of course, the term of their retirement would be much longer. Part of the increase is due to changes in average life expectancy; but in greater measure it is due to the earlier average age of retirement.

Wolfbein notes some of the occupations that show the highest proportion of workers of 65 and over; many of them are comparable with those in the U.K. Thus in 1960 about 10 per cent of self-employed shopkeepers were 'older men', and about 14 per cent of farmers. Among the relatively low-paid jobs that fall into the same category were those of liftmen, porters and janitors. He suggests also that a few occupations, such as those of shoe repairers, smiths and tailors, are failing to attract young labour, and in consequence tend to retain their older employees. It is doubtful, however, whether a proportion of these would not have been in the class of self-employed men, to whom reference was made in Table I above (chapter 1). In one respect there appears to be a considerable difference between the two countries. Wolfbein states that in 1960 some 38·4 per cent of all employed men from the age of 65 upwards were on part-time jobs. In the U.K. in 1961 only about 21 per cent of the employed men in the same age range were recorded as working part-time. The figures may not be very reliable in either case; but they possibly reflect a contrast in social approaches to the problem.

2. *Role of Trade Unions in the U.S.A.*

What has impressed a good many observers is the extent of responsibility shown by some of the larger U.S. Unions in the matter of their retired members—e.g. by the Union of Automobile Workers, the United Steelworkers of America, the Textile Workers Union of America. There has been a volume of published handbooks, guides to self-preparation, journals, etc., as for instance a regular journal *The Senior Steelworker*. Much of the interest from the late 'fifties has been associated with negotiations about modified rules of seniority. Thus Mr C. E. Odell of the U.A.W. stated at the White House Conference on Ageing (1961), 'Despite the adverse criticism of seniority provisions, I believe there is undeniable evidence to show that without such provisions there would be hundreds of thousands, if not millions, of older workers among the nation's current unemployed'. He went on to admit that seniority practices 'may become a roadblock, when the job is wiped out or radically changed, or when the plant moves . . .' This, of course, is familiar experience elsewhere than in the U.S.A.

Odell referred to various newly negotiated agreements on 'mandatory retirement'. In some cases men of 65 could retire if they wished with full pension benefits; but retirement at 68 was mandatory and final. He added that under this agreement there had been few grievances; and it seemed in fact a significant point that 70 per cent of automobile workers retired on their own initiative before they reached 68.[1]

[1] Charles E. Odell, Director of the Older and Retired Workers Department of the U.A.W.

The energies of the Unions have been naturally canalised into efforts to improve social security provisions and especially medical aid provisions. But they have paid some attention to the establishment of 'Drop-in Centres' or Clubs for the use of their pensioners. Here Union branches have been encouraged to form local joint committees, that might be representative of the entire labour movement of the area.

The concern that Union members should prepare their minds for retirement was reflected in an article in *AFL–CIO Education* (1960); it emphasised the need to have trained Union leaders for the purpose. 'The Union Staff Leadership Group must be prepared to step in and help at any point along the road, until the trainee leaders feel secure and comfortable with their newly acquired skill and status as discussion leaders'.

Though some Union branches have further set themselves on occasion to assist retired members to obtain seasonal employment with local firms, there is not much evidence that part-time work on domestic repairs or garden maintenance has been very plentiful. The novel feature (at all events for us in this country) is the degree to which U.S. Trade Unions have been sharing with voluntary agencies in helping to create opportunities for retired members to do social or constructive work of some kind.

3. *U.S. Sociological Contributions*

Economists in the U.S.A. seem to have become reconciled a little earlier than in the U.K. to the fact of a pre-determined age of retirement; in the U.K. we were still then trying to find means for prolonging the average working life. The outcome in the U.S.A. was a growing sociological interest in the meaning retirement is likely to have for those who are involved in it. Anthropological literature was carefully studied for any comparative evidence on the social attitudes towards old age. The facts that apparently emerged are now familiar to most sociologists in the field. Irving Rosow (Western Reserve University,

Cleveland) reviews some of the material.[1] The welfare of the aged, he points out, has varied with such factors as the amount of the resources they could command, the social functions they performed and the general state of social organisation. He suggests that in the most primitive economies, of which we have knowledge, people will retain a man and find a place for him, just about as long as his capacity and productivity match or exceed his consumption.

Rosow adds that at the time of writing self-employment accounted for almost half the older workers in the U.S.A. But the economy itself, he says, is corroding the opportunities for and conditions of self-employment; in the process older people's employment will steadily drop. The same kind of comment has been made by others. Thus Professor Arnold M. Rose (University of Minnesota) remarks that, 'The situation of the elderly in the United States has been especially unfavourable in the last fifty years with the decline of the self-employed occupations and the rise of compulsory retirement'.

One result has been the spread since the late 'fifties of a wholesome controversy about the mental attitudes that can be observed in a retired population. One school inclines to think in terms of an intrinsic 'disengagement', i.e. almost a natural tendency of emotional withdrawal. There comes, in other words, an inevitable, gradual and mutually satisfying process of 'disengagement' from society. It is assumed to be *mutually* satisfying, because society as a whole is gratified when the old no longer interfere with the normal course of economic processes, and because the old for their part can better face the future with equanimity by gradually relinquishing their social ties.

William E. Henry (University of Chicago) supports this theory.[2] He holds that it is a matter of the changing balance between inner and outer events; with age the inner events of

[1] Irving Rosow, 'Old Age: One Moral Dilemma of an Affluent Society', *The Gerontologist*, December 1962.

[2] W. E. Henry, 'The Theory of Intrinsic Disengagement', *Age with a Future*, Copenhagen, 1964.

life take on an increasingly central importance. By contrast, he implies that an actively involved person in middle life experiences much greater 'closeness to others' and much less attention to his own 'inner state'. He compares the mentality of the old with earlier periods of 'negativism' in life, e.g. that of a three-year-old American child and that of the 'selfish' phases of adolescence.

Professor Rose is the protagonist of an opposing school of thought.[1] He contends that this 'disengagement' process is not psychologically inevitable, but rather continues for some people one of their life long characteristics. Moreover, the process is not necessarily desirable. Thus professor Robert J. Havighurst (University of Chicago) has shown reason for thinking that the 'non-disengaged' are on the whole the happiest. Finally, Rose himself believes from his research evidence that this 'disengagement' is simply a function of American culture in the present phase of its organisation; it is in no way universal for all time.

Rose had promoted some sociological inquiries to test his hypothesis. He has meanwhile moved from a more neutral theory, that the attitudes of the old are a product of the varying interactions between older and younger persons in different cultures, to the positive idea of what he terms '*ageing group consciousness*'. By this he means the types of people who are becoming aware, not merely that they are growing old, but that they are subject to certain deprivations because they are old; they accordingly act with some positive effort to overcome these deprivations, and they feel a sense of identification with other elderly persons for this very reason. In his inquiries he compared a number of old people who had joined organisations, the membership of which consisted only of the elderly, with a number of people who had joined no such groups.

All the persons approached were between 65 and 85 years

[1] Arnold M. Rose, 'A Current Theoretical Issue in Social Gerontology', *The Gerontologist*, March 1964. See also his various discussion papers on the subject.

of age; they were resident in Minneapolis and St Paul. It is significant that one of the organised groups from which he took his sample was 'Legislative Goals for Senior Citizens Study Club', a body drawing its members from all the Old People's Clubs in Minneapolis. A growing tendency among retired men to form themselves into political pressure groups has been noticed by several U.S. writers on the subject. In the upshot, Rose felt that there were few sharp differences between his two types of retired persons in regard to the hobbies they had followed before the time of their withdrawal; but the 'group conscious' men had certainly been more inclined to take up sports and games in an active way. The more isolated and 'disengaged' men had fewer continued interests in hobbies. Again, 53 per cent of the 'group conscious' men asserted that they felt younger than their years, as contrasted with only 37 per cent of the rest.

Professor Rose has been among the first to distinguish a gradual movement towards a kind of 'age culture'. 'In the eyes of many older persons', he said, 'the ageing are being transformed from a category to a group. The important phase comes when they begin to talk over their common problems in a constructive way'. That similar trains of thought have been followed in the U.K. will perhaps be clear from Chapter 11.

11 New Approaches to the Retirement Problem

It remains for us to consider what economic and social research will be needed, before we can hope to solve the human dilemma. The industrial conditions, that are continually generating a 'retirement' problem are very complex. But the underlying cause today is this. Technologists have almost reached the stage at which they can immediately translate into machine design the findings of laboratory physicists and chemists; the two parties are, in fact, beginning to talk much the same language. Each new principle discovered can be rapidly embodied in some type of power-driven mechanism. There are of course many forms of human resistance to the industrial momentum of the process; and most of them, when examined, are seen to be reasonable enough. But the time factor is here of little importance, because modern technology (combined with economic competition) must at last wear down all the resistant forces.

Meanwhile, the convenience of a 'retiring age' is the most obvious immediate way of dealing with such redundancies as result from changes or concentrations in a labour force. We have to recognise that the problem is in its essence a new one. There have naturally always been individual men who were unwillingly alienated from industrial employment simply by reason of their age. The novelty to-day lies in the fact that this practice is being accepted by Western societies as a normal state of affairs. The decisive change in public attitudes came in our own Country somewhere about the late 'fifties; it had started a little earlier in the U.S.A.

We must assume, then, that a prolonged period of retirement is becoming as much a social necessity for an older man as had been his periods of schooling and gainful employment.

Half a century ago the age categories were much simpler to define. Only in respect to his entitlement to a State pension had a man's age to be industrially established; and for almost twenty years in the United Kingdom that age had been 70—an age at which the pension might very properly be described as an Old Age Pension. But the widening adoption by employers of a retiring age (usually about 65) has created a category of men who can no longer in most cases be thought of as 'elderly' in the physiological or psychological sense of that term. Where are such men to be rated in the order of social values? What is to be the *positive* content of their lives?

Economic Research

In the field of economics a more detailed analysis will no doubt be needed of the whole concept of a pensions system. Pensioners fall by definition on the consumption side of the national balance sheet. But we have to suppose that most of them (at any rate those from the manual grades of industry) would be demanding only a limited range of goods and services. The range would be specific to their age and to their diminishing family commitments. It has always been assumed, however, that the basic pension *ought* to approximate to an income standard that would accord with modern civilised ideas; the process is admitted to be a slow one, but the ultimate goal is socially approved.

In that case there are at least two economic questions that need to be answered. To begin with we have as yet no scientifically determined standard of sufficiency *based on the cost of living of the retired manual worker*. We should have to start the inquiry by taking it that their outlay would be entirely on commodities and services appropriate to their age. We should then try to find out how on average they would probably spend every proportionate addition to the existing basic pension; and we should have to go on doing so, until at last we reached a theoretical level of consumption that most of us would agree to be consonant with modern civilised standards. That might seem a matter of opinion. But the queer thing is that we have no scientific way of settling what the standard of consumption *ought* to be (allowing of course for price changes) except the time-honoured method of appealing to the judgment of all 'right-thinking' men. To ask what is an adequate pension level is only one remove from asking what is an adequate wage level; and that last is frequently under discussion and decided ultimately by some kind of general agreement among the parties concerned.

We are poorly provided at present with the types of factual and budgetary material we should need for such an estimate of income sufficiency; and that no doubt because the results of an inquiry might if they were implemented lead to a considerable redistribution of incomes. But I can see no alternative at this stage to a complete social survey of the domestic budgets of pensioners, aimed to establish the minimum standard of domestic replacements, repairs, heating, hospitality, means for communication, travel, etc., that a retired man ought properly to enjoy.

The second question we should have to answer is that of the economic source of the pension itself. The precise methods used by a government from time to time for diverting purchasing power from one group of consumers to another is of no great significance; for these are simply the methods it uses to make the burden on the employed and tax paying public seem as light as possible. But is the State pension based on the principle of a kind of universal Endowment Insurance? Or might it perhaps be looked upon as similar to the reserves that an industry sets aside against the wear and tear of machines and plant? Either interpretation could, in theory be valid. The former is, of course, associated with the presumption that those who pay insurance premiums acquire a right in law to a pension that they might not otherwise have had. The latter has the advantage that the pension fund could be collected from industrial undertakings in the form of a levy on the total realised value of goods and services. But in any case, whatever financial meaning we attach to the State pension, it must always involve some re-distribution of the means of obtaining goods and services, in favour of a large and increasing body of pensioners. It is therefore important for us to know precisely *what classes* of goods and services we should have to reckon in their domestic expenditure. We can take it for granted if we like, that their demands would be modest. I could suggest, however, one yardstick of adequacy I should like to see applied; and that is that a man's basic pension ought to be just sufficient to stimulate him, if still active in mind and body, to take up voluntarily any useful pursuits for which he has a taste. It seems to me very possible that there is a level of retired income, below which such a stimulus rapidly declines; a man can become too concerned with his elementary subsistence to feel that work done voluntarily and without payment is worth undertaking.

Social Research

Though the financial and the social aspects of retirement are closely interwoven, it appears to me that an inquiry into its *social content* is likely in the long run to prove the more important. By definition, complete retirement has no place in industrial production; and it is clear, I think, that most of the activities of pensioners would have to be undertaken voluntarily. In other words, they must be prepared to recognise that it will be the exception rather than the rule for their 'work' to attract any payment. This suggests the need to consider to what extent the more vigorous of pensioners will tend to become a conscious 'culture group' in society with their own set of values and demands.

If there is a tendency for what we may call an 'age-consciousness' to develop among retired men, it would, of course, come as a natural counterpart to the obvious age-consciousness shown by modern youth. As a matter of fact, such a thing is probably characteristic of many societies with a fairly stable economy and of those in which a militant sense of class distinctions is for the time dormant. It is, for instance, traditional in various of the tribal communities of Africa; and it may well become a feature of the socialised economies of Eastern Europe. Each age-conscious group insists upon its own cultural rights; that is to say, its members demand the chance and the means to express themselves as fully as is socially possible. It is for symptoms of this kind of demand among retired men to-day, that we should now be looking.

The culture, that is peculiar to a social group, usually begins to take shape well before its members develop a full consciousness of their collective aims and interests. In this case we should certainly examine the growth of a 'club' life among pensioners. Historically the emergence of clubs or associations (under whatever names) has often been the early symptom of a social group's awareness that its members have a common interest. Pensioners' clubs have been instituted under very varied auspices. A large proportion of them are still conceived as adapted mainly for the needs of 'old people'. But the members of several of them are already associating with one another as consciously political pressure groups, while in others they organise themselves for forms of voluntary welfare work or to carry out mutual services. Retired professional men seem more disposed to attend mixed centres that attract also a number of persons who are still occupied with their normal business.

The functions of all these clubs are not likely to remain static. Even the most passive of them might be gradually invaded by a number of the more active-minded and energetic of the pensioners; and their objectives would change in the process. They would become centres of discussion and planning, not only places for entertainment and social intercourse. The demands put forward are almost invariably for more room space, and for the means of carrying on such hobbies, crafts and other interests as the members individually or collectively choose to follow. It has been suggested, indeed, in some quarters that, if the authorities contemplate setting up workrooms for the retired, of the kind mentioned in the last chapter, they would do well to experiment by setting them up within an existing 'club' atmosphere; and the workrooms ought in that case, no doubt, to be largely planned and run by pensioners themselves. The question whether goods produced or processed in the workrooms found a market would be of less importance; and that would be of some advantage, since we know that their purely commercial uses have an uncertain future.

So much for the social *medium* through which such a culture of retired men might conceivably come into being. What would be the *substance* of that culture? It is obvious that, when we speak of activities and interests that have to be pursued voluntarily and without payment, we are touching the fringes of what is often referred to nowadays as the impending problem of 'leisure'. We should thus examine that problem as a whole; and we should begin by inquiring whether men's ways of filling up their leisure time (when they have it) will come to represent some kind of psychological reaction to an industrial world increasingly dominated by mechanisation and automation. That is not as improbable as it might seem. In times of disturbing change the human mind always tends to grope round to find ways of re-establishing its spiritual equilibrium.

It has been reasonably surmised that in that case we might see among other things a long-term growth in the taste for cultivating the handicrafts and the domestic arts and skills. What effect such a change in popular taste would ultimately have on the consumer goods industries it would be hard to say. But if large numbers of householders do acquire the habit of producing and possessing an amount of home-made furniture, fabrics, pottery and metal work there is bound to be some marginal replacement by these products of the factory-made products. The form of spare-time culture I am envisaging would not however, be a mere reversion to mediaeval handicrafts; many men, who have already a bent for this kind of hobby, equip their private workrooms with a variety of hand-power tools. They show considerable aptitudes for selecting and repairing them. This certainly seems one of the more likely characteristics of any coming reaction to our modern industrial trends.

Now, as far as retirement is concerned in this context, we must recognise that comparatively few manual workers to-day would have acquired much skill in the traditional handicrafts, even aided by power tools. We should have to wait for an age of increased 'leisure' to encourage the spread of skills of the kind. But the real point about the active retired men of the future is that they will be well fitted to round off such a domestic culture into an acceptable mode of life. They will be largely instrumental in helping to stabilise a curious hybrid economy based in great part on an advanced mechanisation but partly also on a domestic hand-power craft production. This at all events is the picture that now appears to be emerging in the minds of a few social theorists; it is undoubtedly worth a more detailed analysis.

In effect, what is suggested is that we cannot dissociate the question of how men are to spend their years of retirement from the question of how humanity as a whole will deal with increased leisure. If that is true, there can be no short-term complete solution for the dilemma of the unwilling pensioner. But it does at least show us in what direction to make our inquiries. The assumption is that retired men will become a more conscious and purposeful group in society, and that, as they do so, they will on their own initiative take an active part in the demand for adequate space and means for leisure-time pursuits; and at that stage, of course, they would at last be playing an authentic economic role, since they would be supporting the new productive forces implicit in an increasing popular urge towards handicraft and similar types of work.

There are naturally other fields for voluntary manual or social work, that are worth studying, particularly within the context of increased leisure. If men have a psychological urge to find a counter-poise to the mechanisation and automation they experience in industry, they are likely to show a greater inclination for performing mutual services for one another in more or less organised ways. Under urban conditions that will often be one of the few modes of *active* satisfaction open to them, as compared with the growth of passive forms of entertainment. We cannot say whether there is as yet much of an increase in the willingness to participate in the Welfare Services of the country or in some offshoot of the Services; and if the desire to do so does increase, we may be sure that it will be due less to a stirring of the social conscience than to an elementary need felt by a proportion of men and women to take a greater part in the ordering and managing of their own communal affairs. Once the taste for this has begun to affect the public mind, we could expect to see an accelerating growth of unofficial bodies of many kinds—i.e. bodies concerned with improving local emenities, with the interests of the consumer, with making provisions for the infirm and aged, with advisory services, etc. Plainly a man's retirement from gainful work would be no barrier to a continued interest in such activities.

What it all amounts to is a serious doubt whether the *active* pursuits of men in retirement can be discussed realistically, unless as a gradual extension of the types of activity that 'leisure' will probably stimulate in men of all ages. Meanwhile we have at least a fair prospect of seeing among retired men the beginnings of what I referred to above as an 'age-conscious' culture or pattern of life. These two social trends will presumably merge with one another to impart to retirement a positive meaning and value. At present we incline to look upon retirement as having only a negative quality, that of a mere suspension of work. Since it is impossible to predict what interests and activities the pensioners of the future will be prompted to follow, I think there is little point in surveying the hobbies usually assumed nowadays to be appropriate for the more energetic of them, e.g. gardening, home decorating, the rearing of small animals or birds; and all these, incidentally, would have to be related among other things to the patterns of urban housing we are likely to have in twenty or thirty years' time.

I have confined myself in this chapter to suggesting areas for further research, simply because our first requirement is a great deal more knowledge. The subject as a whole has been neglected; and that probably for a reason I have already emphasised, that this is a borderland or transitional phase of life, the human significance of which is only just becoming generally recognised. We understand of course, the category of 'employment'; and we understand (or believe we understand) the category of 'old age'. What we have not fully grasped is that technological changes are creating an intermediate stage, often one extending to ten or fifteen years of the life span.

In fact, if we are to have any rational policy in the matter, those who are responsible for our affairs must avoid the fallacy of supposing that the moment at which men are retired from gainful employment is identical with the moment at which old age begins. That is no longer true. Broadly speaking, the predetermined age of retirement is the age at which a steadily increasing proportion of men are perceived to be no further capable of meeting the physical or psychological demands of mechanised or automated industry. The onset of old age, on the other hand, ought properly to be defined as the age at which a steadily increasing proportion of men are recognised to need care and provision, either from their families or through the Health and Welfare Services. With the advance of medical science the gap between these two points will tend to lengthen. It is, as I have said, a by-product of economic and technical progress; and society must be prepared to face up to it.

INDEX

Adams and Cheeseman (Northern Ireland), 111
Age structure of industries, 63
Alternative work for older men, 69 ff.
  in manufacturing industries, 70 ff.
  analysis of 'light' jobs, 71
  in non-manufacturing industries, 77 ff.
  availability of, 90
Automation, 39 ff.
  effects for older employees, 101 ff.

Barkin: U.S. unemployment and age, 14, 65
Booth: on the aged poor, 18
Bus transport: alternative work, 80

Census of 1901: numbers 'retired', 20
Census 1921–61: rates of retirement, 34 ff.
Clark: employability in Canada, 74
Coal mining: alternative work, 81
Cole and Utting: National Survey, 115

Economic factors: on retirement ages, 60 ff.
Employability of older men, 49 ff.
  factor of supervision, 51
  in engineering, 52
  in furniture production, 53
  in building, 57
Ergonomics, 38

Ferguson Anderson and Cowan (Glasgow), 120

Havighurst (U.S.), 111, 141
Health status: relation to age, 109 ff.
Henry (Chicago), 140
Heron and Chown: Merseyside inquiry, 56
Hobson and Pemberton (Sheffield), 112

I.L.O.: 'work and retirement', 69

McKeown, Brown and Whitfield (Birmingham), 113
Mental changes with age, 101 ff.
Ministry of Labour: statistics of employment, 26 ff., 32 ff.
  on employment of older men and women, 69
Ministry of Pensions: statistics of retirement, 29, 119

Odell (U.S.): T.U. attitudes, 138

O.E.C.D. Seminar: age and employment, 13
Outwork: for retired men, 123 ff.
  availability of, 123
  in mental hospitals, 125

Parsons (Swansea), 115
Pearson: Liverpool inquiry, 119
Power generation: alternative work, 86
Promotion policies in industry, 64

Rail transport: alternative work, 77
Redundancies: effect on retirements, 62
Rehabilitation policies: effects on 'light' work, 94 ff.
Retirement: definition of the problem, 16 ff.
  historical perspective, 17 ff.
  statistics of age etc., 24 ff.
  attitudes to, 117 ff.
  part-time work in, 130, 133
  social work in, 131
  income problems in, 144
  cultural problems in, 146 ff.
Richardson (Aberdeen), 113
Rose (Minnesota), 140
Rosow (Cleveland, U.S.), 140
Ruskin: on pensions, 18

Self-employed men: duration of working life, 19
Service occupations: growth in numbers, 47
Sheldon (Wolverhampton), 110
Sheltered industrial workshops, 127
Simonds and Stewart (Dorset), 112

Technical factors: in age of retirement, 37 ff., 48
  social consequences, 42 ff.
  manpower changes, 43
T.U.: attitudes on retirement, 61 ff.
  U.S. attitudes, 138

U.S.A.: National Health Survey, 114
  researches on retirement, 136 ff.
  sociological studies, 139

War, 1914–18: effects of, 24 ff.
Weir (Glasgow), 118
Wintringham: Slough inquiry, 55, 117
Wolfbein: U.S. retirement statistics, 136

Zonneveld (Netherlands), 114